"Tod Bolsinger eloquently compares the growth we experience through trials and the crucible of leadership experienced in the midst of organizational change. The strong pull of historical inertia too easily negates forward progress in far too many ministries. Tod's insightful understanding of leadership effectiveness skillfully delves into the core character traits necessary for a leader to prevail through both the rejection of and resistance to transformation. As a thoughtful, innovative leader, Tod's acumen makes *Tempered Resilience* a critical read for every leader seeking to navigate an organization through an ever-changing environment."

Santiago "Jimmy" Mellado, president and CEO of Compassion International

"In *Tempered Resilience,* Tod Bolsinger cuts to the core of why so many gifted leaders struggle in periods of transition and how leaders can position themselves to thrive amid the chaos of change. Full of scholarly analysis and personal anecdotes, this book will both encourage your soul and challenge you to embrace the extensive life transformation that accompanies leadership."

Linda A. Livingstone, president of Baylor University

"Once again Tod Bolsinger has written a book for our times. With his incredible capacity for storytelling that allows principles to shine, in *Tempered Resilience* Bolsinger has spelled out a pathway for leadership and leadership development for this era of unprecedented change. This will become a classic that I'll refer to over and over again."

Jim Herrington, cofounder of The Leader's Journey: Coaching for Wholehearted Leadership

"In *Failure of Nerve,* Edwin Friedman named a crisis of leadership that dominates our cultural context. In *Tempered Resilience,* Tod Bolsinger provides a vision and language for how we address that crisis head on, cultivating leadership not just to survive but to thrive in the midst of change. Built on decades of personal experience, broad engagement with the stories of significant leaders, and keen insight into the intersection of factors and practices necessary for the formation of Christian leadership, this book is indispensable for those who wish to faithfully lead in church and ministry contexts."

JR Rozko, national director, Missio Alliance

"Tod Bolsinger is brave enough to admit that leadership is grueling. If you want to be a good leader, he teaches, prepare yourself for emotional pain, sacrifice, and the very hard work of becoming a more grounded, mature, and humble person. But accompanying this bracing challenge is a refreshingly practical guide to the kinds of disciplines the aspiring leader can exercise to become that kind of person. Those pursuing pastoral ministry will especially benefit from Bolsinger's insights and candid reflections on his own experiences. *Tempered Resilience* is neither abstract nor academic. It's a relentlessly honest book of wisdom from a devoted Christ follower that's meant to be applied in the real world."

Amy L. Sherman, author of *Kingdom Calling: Vocational Stewardship for the Common Good*

"This book stands apart from many others on leadership because it has a strong beating heart of love and hope. There is love for organizations, baffling and stubborn as they can be, yet there is hope that they can grow and heal and transform. It is a book that roots down deep into a biblical and theological bedrock and then branches out into possibility. It is seasoned with realistic, even mournful acknowledgement of the difficulties and griefs of leadership. But for leaders who are discouraged and exhausted, this is, ultimately, a joyful book."

Leanne Van Dyk, president and professor of theology at Columbia Theological Seminary

"With *Canoeing the Mountains*, Tod Bolsinger gave us a practical guide to leading through the uncharted territory of our times. Now with *Tempered Resilience*, Bolsinger takes us into even more difficult and dangerous territory—the leader's own life. Drawing on his long experience as a premier organizational leader and coach, the author lays bare the struggles that block so many of us from greater influence. He then shows us how the very forces that are often the undoing of leaders can become the ones that make us. If you are looking for a resource to propel you to the next level of leadership character and effectiveness, read this book."

Dan Meyer, senior pastor of Christ Church of Oak Brook, Illinois, and chair of the board of trustees at Fuller Theological Seminary

"Tod Bolsinger has written another gift for the church and her pastors and leaders. As the world around us rapidly changes, churches are faced with their own adaptive challenges. The toll that change takes on a leader has the potential to shape the leader for the better. With a pastor's heart and a wealth of experience, Bolsinger tells us how resilient leaders navigate change with grit. Every church leader needs this in their library!"

Tara Beth Leach, senior pastor of PazNaz, author of *Emboldened* and *Radiant Church*

TOD BOLSINGER

TEMPERED
RESILIENCE

HOW LEADERS ARE
FORMED IN THE
CRUCIBLE OF
CHANGE

An imprint of InterVarsity Press
Downers Grove, Illinois

InterVarsity Press
P.O. Box 1400, Downers Grove, IL 60515-1426
ivpress.com
email@ivpress.com

InterVarsity Press® is the book-publishing division of InterVarsity Christian Fellowship/USA®, a movement of students and faculty active on campus at hundreds of universities, colleges, and schools of nursing in the United States of America, and a member movement of the International Fellowship of Evangelical Students. For information about local and regional activities, visit intervarsity.org.

Scripture quotations, unless otherwise noted, are from the New Revised Standard Version Bible, copyright © 1989 National Council of the Churches of Christ in the United States of America. Used by permission. All rights reserved worldwide.

While any stories in this book are true, some names and identifying information may have been changed to protect the privacy of individuals.

Published in association with Creative Trust Literary Group LLC, 2006 Acklen Ave, PO Box 121705, Nashville, TN 37212-9998, www.creativetrust.com.

Cover design and image composite: David Fassett
Interior design: Daniel van Loon
Images: burst of glowing lines: © Baac3nes / Moment Collection / Getty Images
    bonfire sparks: © Malorny / Moment Collection / Getty Images

ISBN 978-0-8308-4164-6 (print)
ISBN 978-0-8308-4165-3 (digital)

Printed in the United States of America ∞

InterVarsity Press is committed to ecological stewardship and to the conservation of natural resources in all our operations. This book was printed using sustainably sourced paper.

Library of Congress Cataloging-in-Publication Data
A catalog record for this book is available from the Library of Congress.

P 25 24 23 22 21 20 19 18 17 16 15 14 13 12 11 10 9 8 7 6 5 4 3 2
Y 41 40 39 38 37 36 35 34 33 32 31 30 29 28 27 26 25 24 23 22 21

TO

MARK ROBERTS

for nearly four decades of

friendship—and formation—in my life

CONTENTS

THE SMITH'S FORGE

*They had become so focused on the aches and pains
in the system that they had been thrown off course by the
complaints. They had stopped supplying vision, or had burned
out fighting the resistance; they had ceased to be the strength
in the system. In short, they had forgotten to lead.*

EDWIN FRIEDMAN

*T*HE QUESTION I FIND MYSELF ASKING is *not* 'Can I learn the skills I need to lead change?' but rather 'Can I *survive* it?'"

The senior pastor of a large church spoke these words to me in a whisper. But I had become accustomed to hearing similar thoughts from leaders in different organizations and in vastly different contexts. In fact, these words repeated over and over again inspired everything you are about to read.

But let me start in two places that are a world—and twenty-five years—apart.

In 1992, my wife and I traveled to Prague, Czech Republic. One day, near the end of our trip, Beth and I walked through Staroměstské náměstí, a large central square. There in the middle of the square were two artisans who were drawing a sizable crowd to watch them ply their craft. They took pieces of scrap iron, discards, and by first heating them until they were soft and pliable, and then held securely on the anvil, they were pummeled and pounded into a new shape. The process repeated: fire, steel, sweat; heating, holding, forming; placed, pounded, and finally, plunged into water.

I watched those artisans—so physical, so purposeful, so violent with hammer and inferno, so precise and exacting. They seemed a living icon of God. For we are the raw material, scraps of hardened, resisting steel. And they, the craftsmen, are so like God in precision and purpose, using the heat of challenges, the anvil of community, and the hammer of practices to transform us from raw material into something useful and beautiful.

Fast forward twenty-five years and travel from Prague to Los Angeles. Adam's Forge is a blacksmithing community in an industrial neighborhood on the north side of the city. It is a place where urban dwellers can leave their cell phones in the glove compartment for a couple of hours and learn the art of transforming rods of steel into tools that can be used. What was once raw material becomes, under the hand of the smith and through the heat of the forge, a new creation that is both pure and mixed, with a new purpose but with nothing lost of its original makeup. Through an age-old process from a previous century, we find a glimpse of what must happen *in our lives if we* are going to be able to lead—and thrive—in leading.

In 2015, I published a book on leadership in a changing world. Since the book was published I have been working at a large theological seminary teaching leadership formation and serving as a senior administrator working on changing theological education. Because of the book and my role, I have spoken about leading change to well over one hundred different groups across the theological and church spectrum in the past five years, and I have heard comments like the senior pastor's many times.

Whether it was speaking to a group of United Church of Christ leaders in a Knights of Columbus Hall in St. Louis, a large group of Lutheran Church—Missouri Synod Christian educators in Phoenix, a select group of Episcopal priests in Manhattan, or Baptist pastors and lay leaders in Auckland, New Zealand; whether Methodists or Pentecostals, nondenominational leaders or seminary educators, over and over someone—usually the person in charge of training, education, or leadership development—would whisper to me, "I don't think we have anyone who can actually *do* this." Indeed, one seminary president said to me, "I don't think I can find anyone *in the entire country* to lead the kind of changes that you are talking about."

The changes that I was describing call for adaptive leadership. And these leaders weren't talking about the specific skills I was teaching. They were speaking about the stamina, the strength of purpose, the perseverance necessary to lead a church, institution, or organization through deep organizational change.

> *"The question I find myself asking is* not, 'Can I learn the skills I need to lead change?' but *rather 'Can I* survive it?'"

Why is this so difficult? *Resistance. Internal* resistance.

Resistance is the key difference between management and leadership: Good management is usually met with a *grateful response* from those whom we manage. Leadership is often met with *stubborn resistance* from the very people we are called to lead.

Management is about helping people get to where they want to go and accomplish what they want to accomplish. Management is about taking care of the most important assets, opportunities, resources, plans, and especially, as one of my colleagues often reminds us, of the people entrusted to our care.[1]

Management, biblically speaking, is called stewardship. And stewardship is about taking care of what is most valuable and accomplishing together what all of us most want to get done.

Whenever I am hiring a youth leader, I often joke that every parent actually wants a youth *manager*. If the youth leader takes ten kids to camp, they want all ten to be brought home safe and sound. As I tell my graduate students, the keyword here is *all*. Bringing home 90 percent is not an *A* in this case.

Humans are wired for stability and continuity, so we are deeply grateful for a good manager who keeps everything running well. But leading change is disruptive. And every-thing within us resists disruption. When we are faced with change, we need leaders who can stand it when we resist the very thing we want and need, even to the point where we will turn on them, oppose them, sabotage them. According to the late Edwin Friedman, one of the critical attributes of a leader who is going to bring about a "renaissance" or renewal of deep change is "persistence in the face of resistance and downright rejection."[2]

Leadership therefore is always about the transformation and growth of a people—starting with the leader—to develop the resilience and adaptive capacity to wisely cut through resis-tance and accomplish the mission of the group. It requires learning and results in loss. And even when we know what we are signing up for, we resist both the vulnerability of learning and the pain of loss. So, to lead, especially in the face of resis-tance, requires that we develop *resilience*.

Resilience is not about becoming smarter or tougher; it's about becoming stronger and more flexible. It's about be-coming *tempered*.

Which takes us back to the blacksmith's shop.

Tempered. Let the word linger there for a moment. What comes to mind? Tempered glass? Tempered steel? *To temper* is an odd verb. It means *both* to make stronger *and* more flexible. Tempered steel is perfectly balanced at the midpoint between too soft to be useful as a tool and so brittle that the tool will break through hard use.

To temper describes the process of heating, holding, hammering, cooling, and reheating that adds stress to raw iron until it becomes a glistening knife blade or chisel tip. It also describes the process by which blending the right ingredients of raw material brings about something greater than the sum of its parts.

> *To lead, especially in the face of resistance, requires that we develop resilience.*

The old King James Version of the Bible uses the word *tempered* (Exodus 30:35) to describe the way an apothecary mixes herbs and spices into a fragrance that is both purer and holier than the original unblended ingredients. Similarly, the soul being shaped for the challenges of leading a people through their resistance needs both hardships and relationships, both hammer and anvil, both forge and pool.

In this book I want to talk about the processes and practices that develop *tempered, resilient* change leaders who will be able to avoid what Edwin Friedman calls a "failure of nerve" as well as what I call a "failure of heart." Tempering a leader is a process of *reflection, relationships, and practices during the act of leading that form resilience to continue leading when the resistance is highest.* It includes vulnerable self-reflection, the safety of relationships and specific spiritual practices and leadership skills in a rhythm of both work and rest.

It is hard, formative work.

BECOMING TEMPERED

One interesting concept in blacksmithing is how *stress* is added to steel to make it stronger. The stress of *forging* the tool and the stress of *using* the tool is the *same*. In this book we will explore a process of leadership formation that occurs while leading. This process is like the way a chisel is forged and then resharpened and retempered over and over again to be a tool for transformation.

Through the lenses of both spiritual-formation texts from Christian theology and leadership development literature from business and organizational psychology, we will find that there is a remarkable overlap in how both ways of thinking understand leadership formation. When those concepts are brought together, the characteristics of transformational spiritual and organizational change leaders reveal a picture of attributes that make up a tempered, resilient leader: one that is *grounded, teachable, attuned, adaptable, and tenacious.*

BECOMING A TEMPERED LEADER

Working: Leaders are formed in leading.

Heating: Strength is forged in self-reflection.

Holding: Vulnerable leadership requires relational security.

Hammering: Stress makes a leader.

Hewing: Resilience takes practice.

Tempering: Resilience comes through a rhythm of leading and not leading.

If the goal of being a tempered, resilient leader is to be strong and flexible enough to withstand both a failure of nerve and a failure of heart, then it is critical to understand that *both* failures are *failures of identity*. And that identity is both revealed—and can be made resilient—in the very act of leadership.

Using the imagery of a blacksmith's shop, the stories of Moses leading the people of Israel centuries ago, and Dr. Martin Luther King Jr. leading the civil rights movement in the 1960s, we will explore the steps in a formational process as *working*, *heating*, *holding*, *hammering*, *hewing*, and *tempering*.

Fire and anvil, Spirit and community are necessary but not alone. For the master Artisan uses anvil and fire with the hammer of hard blows—both *crises* we undergo and *practices* we undertake—to shape, strengthen, smooth, and shine us into something both beautiful and useful. Without the Spirit, the hammer of life's difficulties and tests would only scar and mar us. Without the anvil, the hammer would crush us to bits. But together fire, anvil and hammer, Spirit, community, and hardship, used by the master Artisan,

> *A tempered leader is formed in the act of leading, through reflection, relationships, and a rule of life, in a rhythm of leading and not leading.*

forge us into something stronger and more flexible, *more useful and more beautiful* than we could ever imagine.

This leads us to consider an inspiring moment—and a transparent model—of a resilient leader that we will return to repeatedly during this transformational journey.

TELL THEM ABOUT THE DREAM, MARTIN!

It was August 28, 1963, and the mall in front of the Lincoln Memorial was filled with over 250,000 people. After a long afternoon of stirring speeches, gospel singer Mahalia Jackson sang two spirituals that caused Roger Mudd of CBS to remark, "all the speeches in the world couldn't have brought the re-sponse that just came from the hymns she sang."[3]

A rabbi spoke and then Rev. Dr. Martin Luther King Jr. led into his prepared remarks. The words for this occasion had come slowly to the acknowledged leader of the civil rights movement. Drawing from the deep wellspring of the struggle for black Americans to experience the justice and freedom proclaimed in their homeland, he and his confidantes had worked late into the evening. This speech was not to be just the words of an eloquent preacher, it was a gift of the centuries-long black struggle. This moment was bringing attention to the blood, sacrifice, and courage of so many who had labored in the long fight for freedom for the African-American community. They knew that they would be speaking to a nationwide audience. And they also knew they would be speaking directly to people who had experienced firsthand beatings, jail, being attacked by dogs, and humiliated by neighbors.

Dr. King and his companions had debated which themes to use in what was an allotted five minutes of speaking time. Dr. King himself had spent the night writing in longhand and by 4 a.m. had put the finishing touches on a text that was meant to be both sobering and thoughtful, absent of inflammatory rhetoric, but sternly calling the nation to account for the on-going denial of rights to so many of its citizens.

Dr. King's speech began more scholarly than soaring, and when he stumbled on a line that he didn't think would work, he began to riff off-script. It was just then that the preacher heard the gospel singer crying out from behind him.

"Tell them about the dream, Martin! Tell them about the dream."

Dr. King's associate and speechwriter Clarence B. Jones, who was seated nearby heard Mahalia Jackson's words and saw Dr.

King glance at Jackson and put his notes aside. Jones said to the person sitting next to him, "These people out there, they don't know it, but they are about ready to go to church."

Dr. King launched into the words that have now become hallowed in our American history, "I have a dream."

Using the imagery of Isaiah, one section speaks to the task of bringing change in the face of immense—even centuries-long—resistance and the despair it can cause.

> I have a dream that one day every valley shall be exalted, every hill and mountain shall be made low, the rough places will be made plain, and the crooked places will be made straight, and the glory of the Lord shall be revealed, and all flesh shall see it together.

And immediately Dr. King brings that vision down to the blood-stained soil of 1960s Alabama and Mississippi, and the daunting task ahead of him.

> This is our hope. This is the faith that I go back to the South with. With this faith we will be able to hew out of the mountain of despair a stone of hope. With this faith we will be able to transform the jangling discords of our nation into a beautiful symphony of brotherhood. With this faith we will be able to work together, to pray together, to struggle together, to go to jail together, to stand up for freedom together, knowing that we will be free one day.

Notice the words. *Hope. Faith. Transform. Together. One Day.*

But notice even more the imagery that sits in the middle of this stirring refrain. *With this faith we will be able to hew out of the mountain of despair a stone of hope.*

Hew. What does it take to become the kinds of leaders whose faith enables them to hew stones of hope out of mountains of despair? What is the process of tempering that produces a tool for hewing?

That's what this book is about. Through the use of a black-smithing metaphor and a deep dive into the leadership challenges of Moses and Dr. Martin Luther King Jr., we will discover together a process that enables leaders to become tools that God can use to transform resistance and despair into hope. We will learn together the way that the Spirit works to forge the character and the resilience necessary to become a chisel that can bring transformation right at the very crux of resistance.

> *What is the process of tempering that produces a tool for hewing?*

For me it's also about the way that "stones of hope" become a way for God's sweeping, radical, landscape-changing (*every valley shall be exalted, every hill and mountain shall be made low, the rough places will be made plain*), culture-changing (*the crooked places will be made straight*), life-changing (*all flesh*) justice to be made present in the world.

One of my favorite images from the New Testament is the way that the church, with Christ, a "living stone," is being built— as "living stones"—into a dwelling place for God on earth (1 Peter 2:4-7). We will focus on the hard, humbling work of being transformed from raw material into a chisel that can hew out of mountains of despair stones of hope. We'll light the forge and rest on the anvil and feel the pounding of the tools that are in the Spirit's hands. We'll enter into a process of transformation and take on the tempering that we need.

We will see that when reflection and relationships are combined into a life of deliberate practice, the leader becomes miraculously stronger and more flexible, tougher and more agile, decisive and more discerning, wiser and happier, more content and even more restless for the cause, the organization, the community, the mission to which she has been called.

The raw material becomes *tempered*. The man or woman becomes a *leader*. And—God helping us—the world is changed for the better.

1

THE CRISES OF LEADING CHANGE

FAILURES OF NERVE AND FAILURES OF HEART

The battles the Greek heroes had to fight
were against their enemies.
The battles their Jewish counterparts had
to fight were against themselves:
their fears, their hesitations, their sense of unworthiness.

JONATHAN SACKS

I believe there exists throughout America today a
rampant sabotaging of leaders who try to stand tall
amid the raging anxiety-storms of our time ... whenever
a [group] is driven by anxiety, what will also always
be present is a failure of nerve among its leaders.

EDWIN H. FRIEDMAN

"TOD, GIVE US YOUR PITCH. Treat us as if we are the people who you would ask to fund this if it was a new start-up company."

I smiled broadly. "Glad to do so," I said as I forwarded the PowerPoint presentation to the first slide.

I was in a conference room provided by a law office, meeting with a group of Silicon Valley venture capitalists on a famous street in Palo Alto, California. We were there to discuss a change initiative I had been tasked to spearhead at the seminary where I am a senior administrator. They were not there to fund the initiative but to give me feedback on it using their expertise as venture capitalists and philanthropists.

As I took a deep breath to launch into my presentation, a former McKinsey consultant interrupted, "Sorry," he said. "Before you start just tell us, *who* this new service is supposed to help? Who is your target *customer*, as it were?" We all chuckled. Seminaries, churches, and Christian nonprofits don't often refer to the people we serve as "customers." But I got the point.

"No problem," I said, "Fuller Seminary wants to serve ministry leaders and pastors who want to grow as spiritual leaders and help the people in their churches and organizations grow spiritually but don't necessarily need the expense or commitment of graduate-level education."

There were nods all around the room, so I began.

Twelve minutes later I finished my presentation. I could see smiles around the room as if they were sharing an inside joke. The former McKinsey consultant said, "You have been doing that presentation a lot around the seminary, haven't you?"

"Yes," I responded. "Faculty groups, senior administrators, staff groups from which I am trying to recruit people to my team. Why?"

"Because your presentation didn't tell us why this would help ministry leaders but why this was a good strategy for *the school*. You gave us a pitch that tried to sell us on how your plan would help the seminary, not how the seminary would better serve the church or make a difference in the world."

I could feel my face flush with embarrassment. They were kind, but I knew that a glaring blind spot had been revealed. I also realized how thoroughly I had been influenced by my institutional context and the worries of my colleagues.

Only three years earlier I had been brought to the seminary as both a former alum with two degrees and as an outsider who had spent the past twenty-five years as the pastor of a congregation, leadership consultant, and executive coach. I was supposed to be the voice of the church speaking into and shaping the academic environment in a more formative direction. And while, in my presentation, I had used the language of making an impact on the greater church, I had defaulted— almost unconsciously—to what would help *our institution* and not what would truly help our institution serve the real needs of people.

Back to the conference room in Silicon Valley. The most senior leader in the room spoke up next. "Tod, look, there is only really one thing that matters if you are going to try to lead something innovative: *Does it fix a real problem?*" He continued, "Can you tell us what *pain point* in the world or the church your seminary's new project would be trying to address?"

I still feel sheepish looking back on it now, but these Silicon Valley leaders were reminding me that genuine leadership must be focused on a vision that is beyond the profit, success, or even survival of the institution. *It must be focused on the needs of real people in the real world.*

Very quickly, the conversation with the Silicon Valley venture capitalists moved from what the school wanted me to do to what the world *needed to have done.* And this not only refocused my sense of what was required of me as a leader but also the constant temptation that every leader faces.

In *Canoeing the Mountains*, I defined leadership as "energizing a community of people toward their transformation to accomplish a shared mission in the face of a changing world."[1] For Christians the motivating factor for leadership is *mission*. Christian leadership is fundamentally about gathering people together to become a *community to grow in order to accomplish something that needs to be done in the name of Christ.* That mission is focused on a need or pain point that if addressed would further the redemptive purposes of God in the world. It is the desire to be a tangible, particular, and contextual answer to the prayer of Jesus, "Your kingdom come, your will be done on *earth. . . .*"

> *Leadership is called into action when there is a* **problem** outside *of the* **organization that needs** *to be addressed* **and the organization needs to change** *in order to take on that challenge.*

For most of us this is straightforward enough. Indeed, those of us called to leadership are motivated by words like *transformation* and *mission*. We are eager to make a difference, meet a need, and, if we are people of Christian faith, see God's reign made manifest in our towns, churches, and organizations. Leadership, as my Silicon Valley counselors were reminding me, is called into action when there is a problem *outside* of the organization that needs to be addressed *and the organization needs to change* in order to take on that challenge.

One of the genuine crises of Christian leadership today is how inward focused it is. A movement founded on the salvation and transformation of the world often becomes consumed with helping a congregation, an organization, or educational institution survive, stay together, or deal with rampant anxiety (often all at the same time). It's not enough to turn around a declining church, resolve conflict, restore a sense of community, regain a business's market share, return an organization to sustainability, or even "save the company." The question before any leader of an organization is "save the company for *what*?"

THE CHALLENGE OF ADAPTIVE LEADERSHIP

The man across the table from me was a generous and successful businessman. He had already given a considerable donation to the work my team was spearheading at the seminary, and we were asking him for even more resources.

He looked at me and asked, "So if another seminary asks you to share what you are learning, what will you do? What will you say to them?"

"It's already happened," I told him. "I have already spoken to a dozen or more schools and seminaries. And when they call, we tell them everything. Everything we have learned. Every mistake we have made. Every pothole to avoid. Everything we haven't yet tried. We share it all." We talked about that what he was funding through us was bigger than us. That what we are trying to do in leadership formation is bigger than any one school. Soon we were talking about Elon Musk's work with Tesla and how he had made the plans for the batteries on his electric vehicles an open-source technology, sharing all of the patents so that other companies could accelerate the vehicles that he believed would help fight climate change.[2]

"The real challenge," I said, "is not figuring out the new plans but changing the factories that are used to building on the old plans." I explained that even if we gave every so-called competitor our plans for innovating Christian leadership formation and theological education, they would have to change their own organizational cultures. That is, both the leaders and their organizations need to adapt.

Developing adaptive capacity, that is, the personal and organizational transformation of leaders and their people to apply and adapt their core values in a rapidly changing context, *is the greatest challenge of adaptive leadership.*

Adaptive leadership, as developed by Ronald Heifetz and Marty Linsky, is an approach to organizational problem-solving that starts with diagnosis: *Is this problem something that an expert can solve or not?* Is this something that requires us to apply a solution that already exists, or does it fall outside of our current knowledge and expertise and therefore will require learning (and usually result in loss)?[3]

Adaptive challenges are the true tests of leadership. They are challenges that go beyond the technical solutions of resident experts or best practices, or even the organization's current knowledge. They arise when the world around us has changed but we continue to live on the successes of the past. They are challenges that cannot be solved through compromise or win-win scenarios, or by adding another ministry or staff person to the team. They demand that leaders make hard choices about what to preserve and to let go. They are challenges that require people to learn and to *change*, that require leaders to experience and navigate profound *loss*.[4]

As we shall repeatedly see, developing *adaptive capacity*, that is, *the personal and organizational transformation of leaders and their people to apply and adapt their core values in a rapidly changing context*, is the greatest challenge of adaptive leadership.[5] Groups are hardwired to believe that survival usually means reinforcing the way things have always been. So when an organization feels stress, the default behavior of most organizational leaders is to solve the problems *for* our organizations rather than *change our organizations* for meeting the needs of the world. The result is that instead of undergoing transformation to be more effective in our mission to serve the world, organizations unconsciously reinforce the very status quo that is *not working*.

So, to restore their flagging attendance or lagging donations, churches keep offering the programs they have always loved and try to fill the facilities that they invested in building. Schools want to attract students to maintain the faculty who have come to research within the safety of tenure and the resources of an academic community. Nonprofit organizations that were once an innovative solution to a real problem become, after a time, organizations whose own survival is now the core purpose for being.

> *The default behavior of most organizational leaders is to solve problems* for our *organizations rather than* change our organizations *for meeting the needs of the world.*

But, when a changing world or changing needs require that the church, school, organization, or institution change to keep being relevant to the real challenge that is arising, it becomes clear that the *internal* organizational change needed—and the losses that must be faced by our people to become more missionally focused—is an even more difficult leadership challenge than the external reason for changing. And when leaders experience the resistance of *their people*, failure of nerve or failure of heart begins to take root.

In the Scriptures we see the people of God wrestle with the losses and learning required of them from the very earliest days—and we see Moses struggling to keep the people of God focused on securing the very freedom they have been promised. In Exodus 13, when Pharaoh lets the Israelites go, God leads his people in a roundabout way through the wilderness. Even though they had just been rescued from slavery through God's multifaceted and miraculous intervention, God knows they are not ready for freedom. He knows he can't take them on the most direct route to the Promised Land because it would risk a confrontation with their centuries-old nemesis, the Philistines, and any confrontation may make them "change their minds and return to Egypt." (Exodus 13:17).

As they camped on the Egyptian side of the Red Sea, the word goes out that Pharaoh is coming for them. In a panic they cry out to God and accuse Moses,

> Was it because there were no graves in Egypt that you have taken us away to die in the wilderness? What have you done to us, bringing us out of Egypt? Is this not the very thing we told you in Egypt, "Let us alone and let us serve the Egyptians"? For it would have been better for us to serve the Egyptians than to die in the wilderness. (Exodus 14:11-12).

Moses assures them of God's presence and power that will protect them, and soon they are standing on the opposite shore of the Red Sea, watching the Egyptian warriors being drowned in the very same spot they had walked across on dry land. They see firsthand God's power again, and Exodus 14 ends with, "So the people feared the LORD and believed in the LORD and in his servant Moses."

After ten plagues and salvation at the Red Sea, the Israelites are full of faith and courage; eager to press on to the Promised

Land. They gather in joyful celebration, and Moses leads them in a song of praise of God's power and trust in God's steadfast love. Moses' sister, Miriam, leads them in another song and they set out from the Red Sea. They experience yet another miracle as God turns bitter, undrinkable water "sweet" (no small feat in a desert) and demonstrates again God's care for the people as they drink their fill.

We would think that having personally experienced such a display of power and love that they had written new worship songs to declare it, they would be more resilient when the rough times come. But in the very first challenge, their faith and courage fold like a deck chair.

In Exodus 16, only *six weeks* after the miracle of the Red Sea, we read, "The whole congregation of the Israelites complained against Moses and Aaron" (v. 2). Protestations soon became a wish to return to slavery in Egypt rather than risk hunger in the wilderness.

Six weeks. One chapter of the book of Exodus. That's how long it took for the experience of loss and anxiety to completely crumble the convictions of the people of God on a journey to salvation. That's how long it took for the people to turn on their leaders. That's how long it took for sabotage to take hold.

For Edwin Friedman, who was both a family systems expert and a rabbi, *this is the critical moment in every leadership challenge.* This the test that must be passed to truly bring transformation and change: *to have the resilience to resist one's own failure of nerve and overcome the anxiety-fueled sabotage that comes when leaders take new initiatives.*[6] "The system . . . must produce leaders who can both take the first step and maintain the stamina to follow through in the face of predictable resistance and sabotage."[7]

And, if my conversations with Christian leaders all over the country are indicative, this may be the single greatest leadership weakness in the church today. While many healthy churches are giving faithful witness to Christ across the globe, most leaders have not been trained for the challenge of trying to bring change to churches that need transformation in order to be faithful to their missional calling. And this is true for educational leaders, nonprofit leaders, or any other organization that have stakeholders who were trained for a bygone era. In the now-famous words of Ronald Heifetz and Marty Linsky:

> People do not resist change, per se. People resist loss. You appear dangerous to people when you question their values, beliefs, or habits of a lifetime. You place yourself on the line when you tell people what they need to hear rather than what they want to hear. Although you may see with clarity and passion a promising future of progress and gain, people will see with equal passion the losses you are asking them to sustain.[8]

When a leader raises awareness of the need for change, the natural result is for stakeholders to resist that change and the loss of that change. That resistance soon turns to sabotage.

SABOTAGE IN THE SANCTUARY AND THE SEMINARY

"So, what's Plan B?"

We were midpoint in a capital campaign to raise the funds for a building project at our church, and I was confused by the question. Five months after the infamous 9/11 terrorist attacks on the World Trade Center and the Pentagon, our mostly older congregation had voted courageously, stunningly, faithfully, and unanimously to tear down almost our entire campus and rebuild it so we could better serve the hundreds of young families that were being projected to move into our San Clemente community. We had revealed our plans, candidly talked about the costs, discussed the disruptions that would become part of our church life for several years, and had called for the vote. It had been a landmark moment in the life of our church and a great accomplishment for our leadership team.

"Plan B? Why would we need a Plan B?" I asked.

My business administrator, whom I will call Bob, looked at me kindly. "I know that everyone voted for the plan, Tod. But what if they don't give to it? What will we do if the money runs short?"

Exasperated a bit, I snapped at Bob, "We told everyone the cost and they *voted* for it. They knew what they were doing. Why would that be any different now?"

"Well," he said slowly, "You know, Jay?"

Everyone knew Jay. Jay was considered by most to be the wealthiest man in our congregation. He might have been the wealthiest man in our community. It had been significant when Jay raised his hand to vote in favor of the building plan because most people assumed that if Jay supported it, it would succeed. And secretly, I think all of us (including me) thought that Jay could personally write a check that would cover a huge part of the money needed to be raised.

He continued. "Jay was deeply offended by your presentation. You know, thirty years ago, he personally built most of the buildings that we are now tearing down."

(I *didn't* know. Somehow, no one had thought to tell me that when I was preparing a presentation about our "poorly constructed buildings that cut corners and were now completely out-of-compliance with the city ordinances.")

He only voted for the project because he was embarrassed, and he knew people were looking at him. But when he raised his hand to vote for the project, everyone *assumed* that it was good with Jay and that he would contribute a lot. But now Jay and his buddies were telling their friends that they were all going to give $1,000 to the campaign (instead of the $1 million he could give) so that they could *say* that they supported it. And then Jay told someone, "We will all watch that boy from Los Angeles fall on his ass."

That "boy" was me.

Sabotage.

First, sabotage is normal. Second, sabotage is what usually leads both to a leader's failure of *nerve* and failure of *heart*.

Sabotage is normal. Acts of sabotage are not the bad things that evil people do to stop good being done in the world. Acts of sabotage are the human things that anxious people do because they fear they are losing what little good is left in the world. Sabotage happens every time a leader takes the initiative to start a change process. It's so intrinsically linked to leading change that, as Edwin Friedman has written,

> The important thing to remember about the phenomenon of sabotage is that it is a systemic part of leadership—part and parcel of the leadership process. Another way of putting this is that a leader can never assume success because he or she has brought about a change. It is only after having first brought about a change and then subsequently endured the resultant sabotage that the leader can feel truly successful.[9]

This is true for every leader and in every leadership context. "If you are a leader, expect sabotage," Friedman used to tell his audiences.[10] And indeed, in every change initiative that I have led, I have experience sabotage firsthand. Yes, there was Jay and a congregation that "forgot" to tell me that I was insulting the most important person for a successful building project. And I experienced a two-year effort for bringing change to my denomination go down in flames without a single leader who pledged their support speaking up to help secure its passage.[11] But even today, leading in the face of sabotage is an ongoing challenge in an educational institution that I *love*.

When I was the first appointment of a new and highly respected president at Fuller, the first phone calls I received when I took up residence in my new office were from previous leaders at Fuller who wished me well. When I would describe the initiative that we were undertaking to bring a radical and overdue change to theological education, they would each warn me that they too had once been in my role. They too had been in charge of a new presidential initiative that flourished for a time and then eventually the system had reverted to the status quo. I was taken to lunch by experienced administrators who shared with me stories of other institutions that had been innovative—for a time—before eventually the old guard would raise up and take down the new thing. As Scott Anthony, Clark Gilbert, and Mark Johnson wrote, "the great sucking sounds of yesterday can subtly but importantly pull an organization back to what it was trying to get away from."[12]

> *Acts of sabotage are not the bad things that evil people do. Acts of sabotage are the human things that anxious people do.*

One former executive of Boeing, who has interviewed more leaders of more industries than anyone I have ever met, warned me that most initiatives go the way of the famous Saturn project for General Motors. Saturn was launched in 1985 as a "revolutionary" new car company. An independent subsidiary of

General Motors, Saturn was specifically conceived to be an innovative response to the rapid growth and competition of Japanese car manufacturers. Offering a different kind of car than the GM's flagship brands (Chevrolet, Buick, Pontiac, etc.), by 1994 it was the third bestselling brand in America. By 2010, it was closed. As David Hanna wrote in *Forbes* magazine at the time, "Saturn, a GM company that had great promise in the early 1990s, ultimately failed because senior GM leaders couldn't see the benefits of new ways of doing things and a new kind of organizational culture."[13] Even today, in a time of great disruption and change at Fuller, an institution known for innovation, the threat of reverting to the past is a constant temptation.

What starts as an innovation to create a new market, ends up getting sacrificed for the status quo and to maintaining the very organizational culture that is contributing to decline in the first place. If it can be said that the most often repeated words of resistance to change is "We have never done it this way before," then the corollary must be "And we are going to keep doing it the way that is *not* working, so help us God."

Churches, seminaries, and nonprofit organizations are notorious for saying they need change and then resisting the very leader they called to bring it. One of my consulting clients told me that he called a meeting of the Session (the governing board in a Presbyterian church) and brought them a daunting dose of reality by showing them that at the rate they were losing members and hemorrhaging money they could predict when they would have to close their doors. The pastor reminded them that they had called him to "turn the church around" and bring in new families in what is a community where the demographic trends are in their favor. Convinced that the urgency of the moment would lead to their support of his change initiatives, he asked them for more clear and vocal support.

They all timidly assured him that they would. But later, one older member called him aside "'Pastor, we all know that you need to bring some changes or the church is going to die. It's just that this is *our* church, and while we know it needs to change, we like it the way it is. Could we just figure out how to delay those changes until after *some of us die* first?"

The pastor told me, "I had to explain to them that because they took better care of their physical health than the spiritual health of the church that it was likely that the church would die before they did."

At times of crisis or crossroads of change, anxious relationship systems default back to what is known, believing that it is the only path to self-preservation and survival, even if it means returning to slavery (Exodus 16:3).

For most leaders this is the most daunting and discouraging dose of reality. That was true for Moses too. The former chief rabbi of London, Jonathan Sacks, points out that while Moses faced a hungry and grumbling Israel with faith, conviction, and creativity in Exodus 16, in Numbers 11:4-15, when they complained about the food *yet again*, he was ready to throw in the towel. The challenge is the same, the response of the people of God is the same, the resistance to change is ongoing, and now, even later in the journey, Moses is demoralized that Israel continues to threaten to turn back. He loses patience and grows frustrated with God, brittle in his character, descending into his own pity party, even asking God to "put me to death at once."

Sacks comments on this passage, tying it back to his study of adaptive leadership concepts.

In the first occasion, Moses was faced with a technical challenge: the people needed food. On the second occasion he was faced with an adaptive challenge. The problem was no longer the food but the people. They had begun the second half of their journey, from Sinai to the Promised Land. They had escaped from slavery; they now needed to develop the strength and self-confidence necessary to fight battles and create a free society. They were the problem. They had to change. That [is what makes] adaptive leadership so difficult. People resist change, and can become angry and hostile when faced with the need for it.[14]

Every group I have spoken to in the past five years requested that—whatever else I teach on leading change—I had to include *sabotage*: how to lead through it—and even more—how to develop the resilience to persist in the face of it. Which leads to the second point for beginning this discussion.

> *Failure of nerve is caving to the pressure of the anxiety of the group to return to the status quo. Failure of heart is when the leader's discouragement leads them to psychologically abandon their people and the charge they have been given.*

Sabotage is often the cause for either a change leader's failure of nerve or failure of heart. As I traveled the country talking to different groups, I began to notice that the most important conversation was not in the question-and-answer session in my workshops, but was during the meal with the leader who had invited me to speak to their group. I began to notice the number of leaders who confessed to me that they felt like Moses in Numbers 11 and were beginning to shrink back facing a "mountain of despair." They began to realize that the tendency for organizations to sabotage change efforts by defaulting back to security and self-preservation was contributing to more leaders suffering both failure of nerve and failure of heart.

Failure of nerve is caving to the pressure of the anxiety of the group to return to the status quo. It is a loss of courage to further the mission and a return to Egypt. Failure of heart is the "emotional cutoff" that occurs when the leader's discouragement leads them to psychologically abandon their people and the charge they have been given.[15] If failure of nerve is being too soft and accommodating to lead change, then failure of heart is becoming so hardened and brittle that leading the change process is changing the leader for the worse. It is becoming so angry at God or cynical about the very people that we have been given to lead that soon we are demanding that God relieve us of the burden, or, in Moses' case, "to put me to death."

In a failure of heart, the first thing to go is hope and energy; soon the very empathy and attunement necessary to help a group adjust to loss and resist despair turn to cynicism, and that in turn results in the entire leading-change effort to be quietly abandoned and the leader often with it. As Edwin Friedman writes, "The capacity of a leader to be prepared for, to be aware of, and to learn how to skillfully deal with this type of crisis (sabotage) may be the most important aspect of leadership. It is literally the key to the kingdom."[16]

CONSIDER

When in your leadership have you suffered from either a failure of nerve or a failure of heart? To which are you more susceptible and why?

Resilience in the face of sabotage is the antidote to the leaders' failure of nerve *and* failure of heart. A tempered, resilient leader doesn't comply with the group anxiety to return to the status quo. And a tempered leader does not become brittle and angry or discouraged and disconnected. Resilience is not something that can be mustered in a moment of "rising to the occasion."[17] It is formed over a long period *before* the crisis of testing so that it can continue the transformation *during* the moment of challenge. Like a soft piece of metal that must be transformed into a chisel to hew a hard granite slab, it has to be worked. The steel has to be transformed—forged and formed and *tempered*—so that it becomes strong and flexible enough to, as Dr. King said, hew stones of hope out of a mountain of despair.

In congregations and organizations filled with resistance to the very changes that need to be made to live out even their most cherished values, leaders need exceedingly elusive character qualities. So, as we consider what it takes to forge resilience in the face of resistance, we begin with the most precious—and rare—raw material.

2

RESILIENCE

THE RAW MATERIAL OF
A TEMPERED LEADER

*Tempering is a heat treatment process that is
often used to improve hardness, strength, and
toughness, as well as decrease brittleness.*

RYAN J. WOES, NORTHWESTERN UNIVERSITY

*Leadership is a critical gift, provided by the Spirit
because, as the Scriptures demonstrate, fundamental
change in any body of people requires leaders capable of
transforming its life and being transformed themselves.*

DARRELL L. GUDER

*O*N APRIL 12, 1963, EIGHT RESPECTED mainline clergymen wrote an open letter to their flocks and the large
populace of Birmingham, Alabama, criticizing the "unwise and
untimely" protests "led by outsiders" whose actions "incite to
hatred and violence, however technically peaceful those actions may be," and were "extreme measures" that are not "jus-
tified in Birmingham."[1]

This letter had been inspired by the Good Friday Parade led by the Southern Christian Leadership Conference at the request of local Birmingham SCLC leaders, to bring attention to the lack of real progress in racial equity and justice for the African American community of the city. The letter was an objection by local white clergy to the actions of Martin Luther King Jr., Ralph Abernathy, Fred Shuttlesworth, and other civil rights leaders who had led a march of fifty people dressed in clothes for Good Friday worship services in violation of the law. This act of civil disobedience by black church leaders had been a peaceful response to avowed segregationist and city commissioner Bull Connor, who refused to issue the marchers a required city permit. It was the first time that Dr. King had ever violated the law with nonviolent, direct action.[2]

The civil rights leaders were roughly arrested and thrown into the Birmingham jail. The white clergy wrote the open letter denouncing the marches and civil disobedience, ending their letter with an "appeal to both our white and Negro citizenry to observe the principles of law and order and common sense." A copy of the letter was smuggled into Dr. King's cell, and he responded with his open letter to his fellow clergymen, appealing to their consciences and defending the actions of the protestors. "I must say to you that we have not made a single gain in civil rights without determined legal and nonviolent pressure. History is the long and tragic story of the fact that privileged groups seldom give up their privileges voluntarily."

Throughout his pathos-filled and powerful letter, Martin Luther King Jr. explains that there was a two-front battle raging around him throughout the civil rights movement. On one side were the segregationists who vehemently resisted full equality for African Americans (and those who, like these clergymen, through their silence and support of unproductive political processes were complicit with them) and on the other were those who advocated violence for bringing the justice and equity that was long overdue.

One side saw him as a rabble-rouser bent on bringing conflict to otherwise peaceful communities; on the other side were those who were frustrated at his use of nonviolence and wanted to push for even more confrontational methods. Increasingly he found himself not only demonized by a fearful majority public but criticized and marginalized by a frustrated and increasingly angry faction that was rejecting his philosophy of loving the enemy, of seeking reconciliation, and of the dream of the "Beloved Community."[3]

In the now-famous "Letter from Birmingham Jail," Dr. King describes the strains of this two-front resistance:

> I have tried to stand between these two forces, saying that we need to emulate neither the "do-nothingism" of the complacent nor the hatred and despair of the black nationalist. For there is the more excellent way of love and nonviolent protest.[4]

He shares his frustration with how often segregationists were enabled by complicit "white moderates," who preferred the status quo and the peace and stability that went with it rather than real change.

> I have almost reached the regrettable conclusion that the Negro's great stumbling block in his stride toward freedom is not the White Citizens' Counciler or the Ku Klux Klanner, but the white moderate, who is more devoted to "order" than to justice; who prefers a negative peace which is the absence of tension to a positive peace which is the presence of justice; who constantly says: "I agree with you in the goal you seek, but I cannot agree with your methods of direct action."[5]

But for Dr. King the *most* disheartening of the white moderates *were the white clergy* who criticized the methods of nonviolent direct action as too disturbing to the status quo. For him this was the rejection of his vocational fraternity who shared the same Scriptures and the same passion for the gospel, only to see it fractured by leaders who criticized him and supported through their inaction maintaining the injustice that was the law of the land.

> I must honestly reiterate that I have been disappointed with the church. I do not say this as one of those negative critics who can always find something wrong with the church. I say this as a minister of the gospel, who loves the church; who was nurtured in its bosom; who has been sustained by its spiritual blessings and who will remain true to it as long as the cord of life shall lengthen. . . . Is organized religion too inextricably bound to the status quo to save our nation and the world?[6]

On May 8, 1967, three and a half years after the speech in front of the Lincoln Memorial and nearly four years after the letter from the Birmingham jail, Dr. King was asked by NBC News correspondent Sander Vanocur about his "dream." He responded in a moment of complete candor:

> I must confess that that dream that I had that day has in many points turned into a nightmare. Now I'm not one to lose hope. I keep on hoping. I still have faith in the future. But I've had to analyze many things over the last few years and I would say over the last few months. I've gone through a lot of soul-searching and agonizing moments. And I've come to see that we have many more difficulties ahead and some of the old optimism was a little superficial and now it must be tempered with a solid realism.

He ends that sobering interview with reiterating a call to nonviolence and a commitment "to get rid of this hate and injustice and all these other things that continue the long night of man's inhumanity to man."[7]

A call to a tempered resilience.

RESILIENCE

When we think about resilience it usually falls into two categories: (1) surviving in the face of harsh personal adversity, and (2) bouncing back from a failure or setback and continuing on. But I want to go even deeper.

Resilience for faith leaders is the ability to wisely persevere toward the mission God has put before them amid both the external challenges and the internal resistance of the leader's followers.

Andrew Zolli defines resilience as "the capacity of a system, enterprise, or a person to *maintain its core purpose and integrity* in the face of dramatically changed circumstances."[8] For Matt Bloom of the University of Notre Dame, resilience in the work and life of a leader shows up in both *the capacity to respond to challenges and the capacity to grow and learn from those challenges* at the same time.[9] In other words, resilience is about the capacity to remain steadfastly committed to wisely discerned goals and values when the forces in front of us and around us would seek to compromise both—and we become stronger through the challenge.

As we will see, resilience also requires a much more complex combination of attributes than stubborn resolve or gritty determination. Resilience requires both strength and flexibility; both toughness and adaptability to endure and to bring transformation. *Resilience comes through tempering.*

This kind of tempered resilience doesn't magically appear, it is formed through intentional reflection and practice. So then, this is a *formation* book. Very often in Christian language, formation

Resilience for faith leaders is the ability to wisely persevere toward the mission God has put before them amid both the external challenges and the internal resistance of the leader's followers.

is generalized to mean the growth of a person in the faith to become like Jesus. This is good and necessary, but in this case we're going to reflect on the even more specific goal of *the formation of a Christian leader to be resilient in the face of resistance when bringing change.* As presidential biographer Doris Kearns Goodwin notes, "Scholars who have studied the development of leaders have situated resilience, the ability to sustain ambition in the face of frustration, at the heart of potential leadership growth."[10]

So, the very goal of a leader's transformation is *becoming* someone who can hew hope out of the despair that arises when the circumstances outside and the struggle inside the organization conspire to resist change. When the system wants to succumb to the status quo, the tempered leader has the fortitude to keep the transformational work going. When the circumstances cause others to become cynical and despairing, the tempered leader has the flexibility to adapt and find a way to continue leading. The goal is not just to survive but to thrive, to not just bounce back but adapt and persist in the work that will bring transformation to the organization and result in a change in the world.

Thus, we will begin to explore that transformation in detail by combining the voices of two different fields of study, one historic and the other more contemporary—Christian biblical and spiritual formation on the one hand and the insights of organizational leadership development, and business and organizational psychology on the other.

We will examine the qualities of formation that enable leaders to develop resilience for facing organizational resistance and sabotage. If the key to bringing change in an anxious and fearful system is, in the words of Richard Blackburn of the Lombard Mennonite Peace Center, to "stay calm, stay connected and stay the course," what does it take to be a person who can do so?[11] Especially what does it take to "stay the course" when everyone around us—even our followers—want to shrink back, give up, or simply stop where they are? As Sacks reminded us, "People resist change, and can become angry and hostile when faced with the need for it."[12]

CHRISTIAN FORMATION AND ORGANIZATIONAL LEADERSHIP DEVELOPMENT

A remarkable overlap exists between Christian *leadership literature* and *leadership development literature* from business and organizational psychology that discusses the attributes and characteristics of resilient change leaders. While the nomenclature varies, the characteristics of transformational spiritual leaders and organizational change leaders make up a list of attributes for a *tempered, resilient* leader: one that *is grounded, teachable, attuned, adaptable,* and *tenacious* (see fig. 2.1).

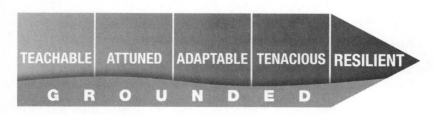

Figure 2.1. The character qualities of a resilient leader

None of these come naturally, and all of these traits are required elements for a tempered leader. In the rest of this chapter and the next, we will explore in detail these characteristics that make up a tempered, resilient leader—one who is both strong and flexible, one who can hew stones of hope out of a mountain of despair. Those characteristics are not linear in development, but they do combine to make up the tempered, resilient character of a change leader.

As leadership studies pioneer Warren Bennis and his colleague Robert Thompson assert, leadership is a "crucible" that "by definition [is] a transformative experience through which an individual comes to a new or an altered sense of identity."[13] Therefore, all of these qualities rest on the primary characteristic that I call being *grounded*: a clear sense of personal identity that is not dependent on the success of the leader to bring change. This grounded identity is the raw material of a leader. As the molecules in steel are both present and changed in both the work of forging and the work of the tool, a leader's identity is both tested and shaped in leadership.

GROUNDED

In the middle of a difficult meeting at the seminary where I serve, when a group of us were struggling to discern the kinds of changes we needed to make and the courage necessary to accomplish them, one of my colleagues, psychologist Cynthia Eriksson, said, "Courage requires a Christian identity of knowing you are loved and affirmed by God, and that your identity is not in your achievements or titles. *Then*, you can take risks and risk failure."

A tempered leader can be resilient and withstand both failure of nerve and failure of heart. Both are failures of identity. Succumbing to a failure of nerve means that our sense of identity cannot take the rejection of the people we have been called to lead, so we join them in their anxiety and enjoy their ongoing acceptance. Experiencing a failure of heart means that we become so discouraged, so brittle and cynical, that we disconnect from the people we are called to lead and abandon— either emotionally or physically—both the people and our calling. Failure of nerve in a leader is an identity that becomes enmeshed with followers and loses something of the independence of thought and conviction; failure of heart is evidenced by a leader who becomes disconnected from followers and gives up the call to care and lead the people they have been given.

To overcome both failures and stay connected to and faithful to the call to lead a people through change requires Christian identity that is *grounded in something other than one's success as a leader* (see fig. 2.2).

Figure 2.2. Resilient leaders are grounded leaders

The speaker at a dinner I once attended was a Catholic nun, and the only reason that this was unusual was that the dinner was a gathering of triathletes at Ironman Canada in 2006. The nun, Sister Madonna Buder, was not there to give a trite invocation before the meal but was a veteran participant asked to say a few words of encouragement to her fellow competitors. Nicknamed "Iron Nun," Sister Madonna would become in 2012 the world record holder in her age group and the oldest person, at eighty-two, to complete the 2.4-mile swim, 112-mile bike, and 26.2-mile run that makes up the Ironman Triathlon.

That evening her message was simple, "Tomorrow, when things get tough out there, remember, you were *loved into existence*. If you get discouraged and want to quit, if you get injured and can't finish, if things don't go the way you hope even though you have trained for this day for months or even years, even then remember: *You were loved into existence*."

A competitor herself with several age-group world records in several running events to her name, she wanted to remind that group of dedicated performers that the most important thing about them was true about them before they had performed at all.

Which was also true about Jesus.

Before there was a single miracle, there was a voice. Before there was a single act of world transformation, there was an affirmation. Before Jesus had done anything for anyone, something was done to and for him. He was baptized in the Jordan River and this word was spoken over him: "This is my Son, the Beloved, with whom I am well pleased" (Matthew 3:17).

While commentators affirm this passage as a kind of inauguration of the work that Jesus is about to undertake as Messiah, it's a subtle but crucial point worth pausing on as we consider what it takes to lead change well: before he had done *anything*, Jesus was already known and already loved and had already pleased his Father.[14]

To be clear, for Jesus—and his disciples—mission and identity are inextricably intertwined.[15] To be a Christian is to be personally engaged in and have as one's life purpose the mission of Jesus Christ. To be a follower of Jesus is to respond to the call of Jesus, and that includes what each of us has been charged to *do*. For a leader like Moses at the burning bush, Jesus at the Sea of Galilee, the disciples as they leave their nets, and you and me as we take up the charge that God has given us to lead God's people, it is of utmost importance, however, to realize that our life of mission and service is always a *response* to God's *prior* love (1 John 4:19).

For Christian leaders who are responsible to bring change and who face resistance and even rejection, a vital, life-giving reality is knowing that *whether we succeed or fail*, our identity as those who are known and loved by God is secure.[16] We are *grounded* not in our success as a leader but, in the words of twentieth-century theologian Paul Tillich, in the love of the One who is the "Ground of Being."

For my own life as a leader, this grounding has been critical. As a young ministry leader who began speaking to groups when I was nineteen years old, it was very tempting for me to find my

> *To overcome both failure of nerve and failure of heart requires that a change leader have an identity that is grounded in something other than one's success in leading change.*

identity and self-worth in my ability to speak well and earn praise from people. There was something both heady and affirming about knowing that I had some gifts and sensing that this was what made me unique or even special.

This also meant that I was very vulnerable to feeling great inadequacy and insecurity when a speaking engagement didn't go well. I cringe today remembering the shame after I told an inappropriate joke to get a cheap laugh from the crowd and embarrassed my friend who had invited me to speak. I remember being so depressed after one speaking engagement where I was alone in a hotel room stewing in my feelings that I had the conscious thought as the temptations swirled within me, *This is how Christian leaders end up addicted to pornography.* And I shudder even now thinking about how the tenderness of vulnerability and the temptation to a particularly nefarious kind of self-comfort could so easily have led me down a painfully destructive path.

I also have such a sense of gratitude for the way that God came to me through people who ministered to me in my insecurities and reminded me that my value was not tied to my ministry success. One evening after a class in seminary, guest lecturer and Vineyard pastor John Wimber offered to have a prayer session for anyone in the class who needed prayer. Even though I was a student, I was already serving as a minister to college students at a church and the ministry was not going as well as I had hoped. I had come under some criticism from collegians who wanted the program to be more social and less about discipleship. A church elder had also stood up in a Session retreat and publicly criticized my leadership. I was deeply discouraged, and when Pastor Wimber offered prayer, I went to the room to receive it.

I remember standing there with my eyes closed and a group of people gathered around me. I heard the voice of a younger man saying in a word that I took as from God, "I love you, my son. I will answer your prayers."

Over and over again through the years, whenever I have been most discouraged I have come back to those words. God loves me as a son, a beloved child. God assured me that even if my ministry wasn't everything I wanted it to be—or even thought it *should* be—God knew the deepest desires of my heart and would meet me in those moments when I poured my heart out to him.

Over twenty-five years later, I stood on a stage in front of over one thousand people at our denominational General

Assembly. I watched the vote tallies indicate that two years of my leadership on a national initiative was being soundly rejected—and this time an eerie calm came over me. This time there was no shame or embarrassment, no deep discouragement, no insecurities that would open me to temptations that could ruin my life. I just remember feeling sad at the result, and then I remember saying to myself, *I'm going home to my family, my church, and my friends. This vote doesn't change anything about that.* As I left the assembly hall, I received a text from three friends, "Come join us for lunch, Tod, we want to be with *you*."

As we will continue to explore, this sense of grounded personal identity and security does not come without years of reflection, deep relationships, and spiritual practices. It is not only a cornerstone of Christian discipleship but serves as the basis of two qualities that must be developed within leaders to enable them to bring change: *vocation* and *differentiation*.

VOCATION AND DIFFERENTIATION

Ruth Haley Barton describes the moment in a leader's life when a "calling" no less definitive, if not as dramatic, as Moses' burning bush beckons us to respond.

> Somehow we know that this moment is different. This is not about making a brilliant career move. It is not about security. It is not about success or failure or anything else the ego wants for us. It is not about choosing among several attractive options. This is about the Spirit of God setting us on our feet and telling us, "This is yours to do."[17]

Christians describe moments like this (whether it is a sudden lightning-bolt experience or a subtler process of being slowly formed to hear the invitation of God) as the call of God on one's life and often the very purpose of one's service.[18] And while the concept of vocation or calling is tied much more clearly to discipleship (and applies to all Christians) than leadership (and to select persons), the sense of calling or *purpose* is critical to leadership resilience in both Christian formation and organizational leadership literature.[19]

In Christian circles, when faced with the daunting realities of facing the disappointment and resistance of one's congregation or colleagues, strong leaders have remarked to me that the only thing that has kept them going was the conviction that "This is my call. This is my assignment. Whether it succeeds or fails, this is *mine* to do."

That conviction of being called by God—and the paradox of being known, loved, and grounded in that love *before* one's assignment—resonates with what psychologists and organizational leaders have discovered creates the foundation for building resilient leadership character.

Adaptive leadership pioneer Marty Linsky calls it "a sense of purpose" that is essential for leading people through the difficult reality of the need for change.[20] The combination of being able to see and accept a difficult reality *and find meaning and purpose in it* has been at the core of some of the most inspiring tales of resilience.[21]

James Stockdale and what is now known as the Stockdale Paradox comes from his experience as a prisoner of war for seven years during the Vietnam War. The Stockdale Paradox, made famous in Jim Collins's book *Good to Great*, is about confronting the "most brutal facts about your current reality" and at the same time finding a sense of purpose and meaning because you believe that you will prevail by turning this into the defining event of your life that will make you a better person.[22]

Lynn Ziegenfuss, former vice president of leadership development for Youth for Christ/USA and a spiritual director and consultant, shared with me that for many leaders the grounding they need to stay resilient in the most difficult moments is knowing *both* that this challenge is their calling *and* believing that something important was being formed within them that God could only do through this leadership challenge. When doing spiritual direction with leaders she is developing, Ziegenfuss says she always asks them to repeatedly and reflectively consider, "What do you think that God is doing in your life that requires that you take on this leadership challenge?"

> *"What do you think that God is doing in your life that requires that you take on this leadership challenge?"*

Viktor Frankl's classic reflection on those who survived Nazi concentration camps, *Man's Search for Meaning*, has become a standard resource for resilience coaching. Frankl observes, "We must never forget that we may also find meaning in life even when confronted with a hopeless situation, when facing a fate that cannot be changed."[23]

When a Christian leader's identity is grounded in the love and the call of God, secure in believing that—even in this moment of challenge—God is completing the "good work" within us and in our organizations (Philippians 1:6, cf. Philippians 2:13), then identity, security, purpose, and meaning are assured even when we face failure, resistance, and rejection. That grounded identity enables the fundamental capacity of a resilient leader to be both distinct from and connected to the people we serve and lead. It's what family systems theorists call "self-differentiation." Edwin Friedman explains:

Someone who has clarity about his or her own life goals, and, therefore, someone who is less likely to become lost in the anxious emotional processes swirling about. I mean someone who can be separate while still remaining connected, and therefore can maintain a modifying, non-anxious, and sometimes challenging presence. I mean someone who can manage his or her own reactivity to the automatic reactivity of others, and therefore be able to take stands at the risk of displeasing.[24]

The key part of Friedman's definition is the ability "to risk displeasing . . . while still remaining connected" to the very people we are called to lead. Since differentiation is "the ability to be fully yourself while being fully connected to people," then differentiation, as part of the grounding of identity enables "the courage to lead people to a difficult place while still being deeply connected."[25]

Since, as Bennis and Thomas point out, the challenge of leadership is a crucible that shapes or even transforms the identity of a leader, having a self-differentiated and grounded identity is the foundation for being a resilient change leader. Indeed, the other four attributes (teachable, attuned, adaptable, and tenacious) are all built on that foundation. Like the quality of the steel that is going to be turned into a chisel, without a strong, clear, grounded identity, a resilient tempered leader cannot be forged.

CONSIDER

In what ways have you experienced leadership challenges as challenges to your identity?

But what if you honestly struggle with having a grounded identity? What if you know that you are sensitive to the approval of others? Business leader and author Terry Looper describes his own challenge with what he calls "people pleasing" and views it as in direct conflict with the ability to hear God's voice and follow God's leading.[26] Or what if you know that you are prone to cynicism and disappointment that causes you to distance yourself from others or struggle to find the energy to take the risks necessary to lead?

My answer to you is good news. Literally *the* good news—the gospel. The answer to our struggle with having a grounded identity is to remember that our identity is given to us by God in Christ. We are a new creation (2 Corinthians 5:17) whose very life points to the hope of all of creation being renewed. For Martin Luther King Jr., standing on the steps of the Lincoln Memorial and listening to the whispered encouragement of Mahalia Jackson, it is the words of Isaiah 40 and the promise of the new creation that enabled the civil rights leaders to continue to labor for decades to hew hope from despair.

The good news of God is that we are loved before we have accomplished anything. We are loved into existence. Nothing can separate us from the love of God in Christ Jesus, and—even if we fail in our leadership efforts, as we surely may—God's love for us never fails. God will complete God's own work in us, and someday the justice will roll down and the kingdoms of this world will become the kingdoms of our God and of his Christ and he shall reign forever.

Let this truth transform you. Let this deep truth deepen you. Let the love of the "Ground of Being," ground you. Give your not-nearly-as-grounded self to the process of transformation into a tempered, resilient leader and trust God for the outcome.

3

WORKING

LEADERS ARE FORMED IN LEADING

A crucible is, by definition, a transformative
experience through which an individual comes
to a new or an altered sense of identity.

WARREN BENNIS AND ROBERT J. THOMAS

Leadership is disappointing your own
people at a rate they can absorb.

RONALD HEIFETZ AND MARTY LINSKY

MY WIFE, BETH, AND I were looking for the location of a blacksmithing class, but there hadn't been a horse in need of shoeing here in over one hundred years. We were not in a place where one would expect to find a blacksmith, but in an urban, industrial area marked by imposing and façade-less buildings ringed by barbed wire–topped fencing.

As first-timers looking for a "Discovery Class," Beth and I nervously drove into the cul-de-sac, continually checking the instructions that had been sent to my mobile phone. We found the makeshift sign and rolled back the heavy gate, drove through and went around a dark corner. We followed a light to an open garage door and hoped that we were in the right place.

A dozen forges raged with fire, all with heavy anvils in front of them. The mix of tools on the wall and in the carts; the grinders and benches, the racks of aprons, gloves, and goggles, and the ubiquitous warning signs made two things perfectly clear:

This was where serious work was done.

And if you weren't careful, you could get seriously hurt.

Beth is an artist who not only works with paint and printing presses but also blowtorches and potentially toxic materials. She wears a gas mask and heavy gloves as often as a painting smock. This was her kind of place. If I, however, am ever making something, it is usually out of words on a laptop computer. I was definitely *out* of place. But here we were entering into an urban blacksmithing shop to learn to make something useful out of steel.

The instructor greeted us, and after signing paperwork that warned us that losing life or limbs was a possibility, he gave us earplugs and then placed us so close to one of the fiery forges that we could feel the heat. Before he said anything else to us, before we even had so much as a full safety lecture, he told us to take a pair of tongs, grab a piece of steel, and put it in the forge.

And just like that, we were smithing.

HEWED FOR TRANSFORMATION

This shop, this process, and the feelings of excitement and dread, anticipation and fear, possibility and danger are an appropriate backdrop for exploring the way leaders become tempered for the work of leadership. If, as Andrew Zolli writes, "resilience is the capacity . . . of a person to maintain [one's] core purpose and integrity in the face of dramatically changed circumstances," then what is the process that forges that resilient character in the life of a leader?

Blacksmithing serves as a perfect metaphor for the long, hard, repetitive, seemingly violent method of transforming a leader. If the purpose of a transformational leader is to hew stones of hope out of a mountain of despair, then we would expect that process to be as transformative for a leader as the process of taking steel and shaping it, hardening it, and tempering it to become a tool that can stand up to both the pounding of the task and the resistance of the rock.

Like the steel we had come to shape, for leaders to take on the characteristics of resilience that will enable them to hew hope from despair, there is a long process of heating, holding, hammering, and tempering ahead *that begins even before leaders know it or recognize it as such.*

Leaders, like tempered tools, are only shaped in the shop. They are only forged in the furnace. They are only made in a place like this filled with both serious work and potential danger. And just as we can't learn to blacksmith or be forged like steel from reading a book or from sitting on a bench, we can't learn to lead without entering into the actual place where the work gets done.

This leads us to the first of two critical introductory points: *Leaders are formed in leading.*

BECOMING A TEMPERED LEADER

Working: Leaders are formed in leading.

Heating: Strength is forged in self-reflection.

Holding: Vulnerable leadership requires relational security.

Hammering: Stress makes a leader.

Hewing: Resilience takes practice.

Tempering: Resilience comes through a rhythm of leading and not leading.

There are books we can read, courses we can take, lessons we can learn through lectures and conversations. But the tempered, resilient leader is forged only in the *process of leading that adds stress to the raw material of our lives*. Which is why it is so difficult and feels so dangerous.

In my conversations with leaders and with those called to train and teach leaders, there has become a common refrain, "How come I can be so good at my job one minute and so completely disoriented the next?" One minute you are the star salesperson, the accomplished assistant, the contributing and valued team member, and then the next minute you are promoted into a leadership role. It is not like it came out of the blue—you have likely been preparing for this next step in your career development. Even more, you may have thrived in one management role only to falter when the demands of change became even more intense, when the resistance to change became more resolute, or when the lack of capacity of a people to change became more evident and exposed.

You wonder why your previous experience or education fails you in this particular crucible. You may even have undergone significant education, perhaps even earned a master's degree, or completed a leadership-development program. (So why do I feel like I am drowning the minute I dive into a new leadership role?)

A 2014 study by McKinsey analyzed why so many leadership-development programs ultimately fail. Their two leading critiques focused on the tendency for leadership programs to devalue the power of the leadership context and the tendency to "decouple reflection from real work." When the standard development experience (usually in an off-site, university-like setting) is divorced from the context and challenge of the work that one is leading, "burgeoning leaders, no matter how talented, often struggle to transfer even their most powerful off-site experiences into changed behavior on the front line."[1]

The problem with most leadership programs, this and other studies have concluded, is that they are focused more on concepts than *context*, principles than *practices*, more on reading experts than *reflecting on themselves*, and, mostly, more on learning *about* leading than actually doing the work of bringing organizational change.[2] They are perfect experiences for the star student, the brilliant engineer, or the sharp salesperson who wants to impress the higher-ups and get a promotion. They are exactly the kind of environment that religious leaders who have a tutored capacity for study and love for theological discussion and historical details thrive in. They create an alphabet soup of acronyms and mnemonics for a long list of leadership principles that can be memorized, tested, and repeated back in papers and on exams.

Studies show, however, that those same concepts are quickly set aside once the leaders enter back into their context, which is always a complex "system of interacting elements."[3] Those principles get lost in the actual practice of leadership and the demands of competing stakeholders. Thousands of pages read become a jumble when anxiety causes us to stop doing the work of deep reflection. In the heat of demands, deadlines, diminishing budgets, and organizational resistance, the stress of the moment results in a *defaulting back* to old habits and organizational behaviors, and that alone is the very failure of leadership that the training was supposed to overcome. Defaulting back to the emotion-laden, deeply unconscious, and stubborn status quo (what Ed Friedman called "the persistence of form") is why so many subject matter experts, students of leadership theory, brilliant engineers, star salespeople, and charismatic associate pastors fail when they get the long-coveted promotion to group manager, project overseer, or senior pastor.[4]

When the focus of the leader is on concepts instead of context, and when resistance leads to a lack of reflection, very soon the swirl of anxiety that accompanies organizational challenges leads to the *failure of nerve* and *failure of heart* that occurs when resilience has not been developed for the leadership challenge.

This is not a new insight. Most observers of great and transformative leaders have always known that leadership skill is developed not in the classroom or from the secure area of one's everyday tasks but embedded

> *Leaders are formed in leading. Leadership formation is a hard and humbling, repetitive process of personal transformation.*

in a context and embodied in practice amid the challenges of leadership and adversities of life. "It is not in the still calm of life, or the repose of a pacific station, that great characters are formed," Abigail Adams wrote to her son John Quincy Adams amid the American Revolution. "The habits of a vigorous mind are formed in contending with difficulties. Great necessities call out great virtues."[5]

The "great necessities" of crisis or adversity in the act of leadership, Warren Bennis would insist, are the crucibles that form leaders.

> One of the most reliable indicators and predictors of true leadership is an individual's ability to find meaning in negative events and to learn from even the most trying circumstances. Put another way, the skills required to conquer adversity and emerge stronger and more committed than ever are the same ones that make for extraordinary leaders.[6]

This leads to the second introductory point: the forming of a resilient leader that occurs amid the very demands of leadership is an ongoing, intense, repetitive, and humbling process of personal transformation.

Whether it is Dr. Martin Luther King Jr. trying to hold together a coalition of civil rights organizations on one side and contend with the vitriol of racist structures and attitudes that have oppressed his people for four hundred years on the other, a nonprofit leader trying to keep offering vital services when government funding has run out, or a pastor leading a congregation to care more for their neighbors than their own preferences while the church is hemorrhaging members:

- Leaders are formed in leading.
- Leadership formation is a hard and humbling, repetitive process of personal transformation.

THE CRUCIBLE OF CHANGE

What makes leadership so daunting, in the final analysis, is the burden of responsibility for the flourishing or faltering, the success or failure of an organization, community, or movement that has been entrusted to your stewardship. *When the challenge of the moment moves from maintaining and preserving to changing and thriving, the stakes are raised and the heat is turned up.* The weight can begin to squeeze the air out of one's lungs. Once we realize that we are facing a challenge that, if it fails, other people will be profoundly impacted, a leader must learn to face that reality head-on. This was as true for Moses in leading the people of God to freedom as it is for a pastor leading a congregation to a new day of mission. Jonathan Sacks writes about Moses before Pharaoh:

We sense the pressure Moses is under. After his first setback . . . he turns to God and bitterly complains: "Why, Lord, why have You brought trouble on this people? Is this why You sent me? Ever since I went to Pharaoh to speak in Your name, he has brought trouble on this people, and You have not rescued Your people at all" (Ex. 5:22–23). In [this passage] even though God has reassured him that he will eventually succeed, he replies, "If the Israelites will not listen to me, why would Pharaoh listen to me, since I speak with faltering lips?" (Ex. 6:12). There is an enduring message here. Leadership, even of the very highest order, is often marked by failure.[7]

It is important to note that perhaps the most important concept to grasp about the formative process of leading is that it is not necessarily—or even mostly—connected to a leadership *role*. Leadership is an action, a function, a particular way of focusing one's effort and attention to the functioning of a group so that they will "tackle tough challenges and thrive."[8] Leading is not about a title, authority, or position in an organizational chart.[9] *Leadership is about bringing change*—in whatever role you occupy.

No matter what position we fulfill in an organizational system of any kind (including any group, congregation, family, neighborhood) if we assume responsibility for bringing change, and if that change requires people to change—and will require us to change—*then* we are leading.[10]

- Every time we step into a space where transformation is both required and resisted, we are leading.
- Every time we step toward a challenge that requires that others step up with us, we are leading.
- Every time we join with others in a cause that requires still more to join our cause, we are leading.

- Every time we embrace conflict as a means to deepen understanding and strengthen connection, we are leading.

- Every time we take responsibility for our actions and face the reality that others will shirk their responsibilities, we are leading.

- Every time the change that is needed in the world requires us to change ourselves, we are leading.

And the key difference between leadership today and leadership roles of the past is that the frequency and speed of change mean that leaders are almost constantly in a crucible moment. Where at one time a specific crisis was the crucible that shaped a leader, today that crucible is the constancy of change. Change requires us to learn from past lessons, insights, values, behaviors, and commitments, and discern which to discard and which to adapt and then apply those new lessons, insights, values, behaviors, and commitments to the present challenges in new—and risky—ways.

If you are responsible for bringing change, and if that change requires people to change—and will require you to change— then you are leading.

STRESS OF THE WORK, STRESS OF PREPARING FOR WORK

In blacksmithing, steel is forged into a tool by the addition of *stress*. High heat, hammering, even the use of the tool itself adds more stress to the steel. Indeed, the very same microscopic process that transforms the steel into something that can *become* a tool occurs when the tool is used. Every time that a hammer and chisel are used on a stone, every time that a pick is used in a mine, every time that an ax is used to chop wood, more stress is added to the tool. And stress is what makes the tool stronger, harder, tougher—and more prone to breaking. *Too much stress* and the very same tool that was cutting stones out of a chunk of granite crumbles under the pounding. For a leader, there is a similar process. *Stress, when handled well, makes the leader stronger.*

Writing about four US presidents who are known for their leadership accomplishments, Doris Kearns Goodwin notes that while we don't know why some leaders fold in moments of adversity, "others, through reflection and adaptive capacity, are able to transcend their ordeal, armed with a greater resolve and purpose." She notes that the challenges Abraham Lincoln, Theodore Roosevelt, Franklin Roosevelt, and Lyndon Johnson faced were daunting enough that "all of them would fall into depression and consider leaving public life."[11] The fact that they faced such ordeals and were able to draw upon those moments as reservoirs of leadership character and resilience is indicative of their capacities as leaders. Even more profound are the ways they allowed those crucible moments to develop within themselves the qualities that were needed most for becoming resilient leaders.

But specifically *how*? How are leaders formed *by* leading and in what ways are leaders specifically formed *in* leading? By adding to a grounded identity, four attributes come specifically *through* the work and *for* the work of leading.

If the foundational characteristic of a tempered, resilient leader is a grounded identity, then the first two characteristics that must be built on that identity are being *teachable* and *attuned*, that is, the *humility to learn* as we go and the *capacity to listen* to those who are going with us (see fig. 3.1).

Figure 3.1. A grounded leader must become teachable and attuned

In other words, as soon as we have a strong sense of who we are and what we are about, the demands of leadership challenge us to be open to where we are wrong and where we must be able to grow as leaders to consider that we may be missing the deeper emotional processes that are at work.

TEACHABLE

As soon as I hit the "send" key, I felt nervousness set in. I worried that my request would reveal that I had such a glaring weakness that it would make others doubt my capacity to lead. I had just written to an old mentor, Steve Yamaguchi, to ask him to take a role in my life that was different for both of us. Steve is an experienced religious leader who has served as a pastor of multiple congregations, as a regional executive, on boards of colleges and seminaries, and in a senior role in higher education administration. I told him that I had some professional development funds at my disposal and that I was committed to being in some kind of coaching, spiritual direction, or psychological therapy to continue my growth as a leader. I also told him that some recent leadership challenges had me feeling that I could use some help in a very particular area of his expertise.

Through emails and personal conversations, I explained.

As you know, I'm a 50-something white guy with three academic degrees who was given leadership responsibility at an early age. I went to seminary on a full-ride scholarship paid for by the church that hired me at 23 to run their college ministry and I became a senior pastor at 33. Most of my work the past two decades has been in pretty culturally white contexts and now I find myself back in Los Angeles in a much more diverse setting with many voices challenging the white normativity that I have to admit that I can't always see and unconsciously assume. I'm wondering if you could become my coach for developing my *cultural competency* (a term that I have heard some of my colleagues use).

This was a sensitive subject for me. I don't like feeling incompetent. It feels embarrassing, even with someone that I have known for years. I felt exposed. Back when I was a younger leader, I had learned the art of how to "fake it 'til you make it," and now I was admitting to someone that I deeply admire that I couldn't fake this one. My colleagues—even my students—had begun to reveal to me how the implicit biases shaped by my lack of awareness about my cultural identity was affecting my capacity to lead well in more diverse arenas. The leadership book that I had written had now taken me into settings where many of my assumptions about leaders and leadership were being challenged as normative for the white majority culture but inadequate for leaders of color, for women, and for settings that were questioning the assumptions of power and privilege. I had faced the fact that I needed help, but admitting it to anyone else—even a trusted mentor—was difficult.

I was relieved when within hours, I received from Steve a kindly reply. "That sounds very interesting," he wrote, "let's talk about how I can be of help." He then went on to suggest one change. "Yes," he said, "you are a 50-something white guy with academic degrees and all the rest. So, let's not assume that I can coach you into cultural competence. Frankly, I don't believe you will ever be culturally *competent,* but we can talk about developing cultural *humility.*"

He explained, "Competence assumes the acquisition of skill and knowledge that will leave one armed with tools to succeed in multiple and diverse settings. The problem is that the world is far too complex to be mastered like this. Cultural humility does not seek mastery of all things cultural, but seeks to develop a posture of life-long learning rooted in self-awareness, attentiveness, and increased capacity for discerning differences as well as similarities." He sent me some resources on cultural humility and encouraged me even to look over the biblical words for *competency* and *humility.*[12]

Competency is only used once in the New Testament and that is with a warning that our true competency is found only in God (2 Corinthians 3:5). But humility is a virtue that shows up throughout the New Testament in multiple verses of exhortation (Philippians 2:3-4) and is a key characteristic of leadership.

Ah. Not competence, but *humility.* Steve was coaching me, and we hadn't even started yet.

If the act of leading is the prime context for leadership formation, then without question the challenge of leadership causes us to confront our need for humility. As Sacks writes, "Leadership demands two kinds of courage: the strength to take a risk, and the humility to admit when a risk fails."[13] The social context and the failures of my trying to lead in my particular context caused me to pick up the phone and call a coach. Acknowledging that the strategies that had once worked in one more culturally homogeneous context were failing in a new context caused me to reach out for help.

While I will say more about the importance of a leader growing in self-awareness about cultural identity and how those dynamics shape leadership, I want to highlight here that the answer to my incompetence was not to assume that I could become competent (indeed, there is a biblical warning about even thinking that way!) but instead to accept the challenge of being an even more humble *learner*.[14]

Humility or *teachability* in both biblical formation writings and organizational leadership development literature is practically a sine qua non of leadership. The highest praise of the greatest leader in the Hebrew Scriptures is that he was "very humble, more so than anyone else on earth" (Numbers 12:3),[15] which in leadership translates into the capacity to learn.[16] Healthy organizations are led by people with a capacity to "learn from others" and this is even truer in environments that are changing rapidly and require a diversity of perspectives, skills, and people with differing life experiences.[17] If the goal of a great organization is attracting and retaining the best talent, the key is to develop more humble bosses. According to one study cited in the *Wall Street Journal*:

> Humility is a core quality of leaders who inspire close teamwork, rapid learning and high performance in their teams, according to several studies in the past three years. Humble people tend to be aware of their own weaknesses, eager to improve themselves, appreciative of others' strengths and focused on goals beyond their own self-interest.[18]

The emphasis, again, in this and other research is *not* that humility is marked by a self-effacing attitude but by the eagerness to learn. Even in interviews with job applicants, dynamic companies are now looking for managers who can demonstrate the capacity to continue to learn, including and especially from their mistakes or failures. One senior executive responsible for hiring for the outdoor clothing line Patagonia asks applicants in interviews to tell him about a time when they experienced a major failure. "If they say, 'Wow, let me think about this, because there are a lot of times when I've messed things up,' that says a lot," he says. *If they have to pick among a lot of humble learning moments, that's good."*[19]

Which takes us to the next characteristic of a tempered, resilient leader.

CONSIDER

When you think of a humble leader you have known or served with, who comes to mind? What was the impact of their humility on you?

ATTUNED

If resilience begins in a grounded identity and a teachable attitude that is humble and open to the perspectives of others, then the next characteristic of a tempered, resilient leader is the capacity to *attune* to others. In other words, if tempered leaders require a grounded *self* and a humble *heart*, they also need an attuned *brain*.

Literally.

Perhaps no research has made more of an impact on the development of leaders in the past twenty years as the discovery and application of *mirror neurons* in the human brain. Mirror neurons are the cells in the brain that fire or interact with other cells when a person acts or *sees another person* act in the same way.[20] In other words, when one person "mirrors" back the behavior, words, or feelings of another person, both brains begin to fire in a similar pattern, creating an experience of connection. Like lovers who complete each other's sentences, friends who break out laughing at just the mention of a shared joke, teammates who can anticipate each other's action for a no-look pass or colleagues who "just know" what a partner would do in the same situation, there is ample evidence that this kind of connection is not just emotional but *emotional* and *biological*. When humans *feel* similarly, they begin to *think* together.[21]

This capacity, often called emotional intelligence or EQ, is often compared to intellectual intelligence or IQ. While IQ is assumed to be fixed at a rather early age, EQ can be developed in people and makes the greatest difference in the performance and capacity of a leader.[22] In his groundbreaking work applying emotional intelligence to leadership, Daniel Goleman found that "nearly 90 percent of the competencies that distinguished outstanding performers was attributable to emotional intelligence factors rather than purely cognitive abilities."[23] And as one group of church consultants concluded, "The emotional competencies of pastors and church leaders are probably the most important factors in pastoral effectiveness."[24]

The cornerstone of emotional intelligence—self-awareness that leads to empathy with others—is so powerful because, in the words of Brené Brown, "Empathy fuels connection."[25] For leadership development theorists, the impact of this insight is almost impossible to overstate. In a rapidly changing world, the ability to work well with people and teams of people is becoming more important than any technical know-how. Even Google, with its capacity to hire the smartest individual players, conducted a famous study where they "reverse engineered" the best teams in order to create the algorithms that would help them learn how to create good teams at scale. (A very googly thing to do!). What did they discover? Great teams run on "psy-chological safety" that is built through empathy, good listening, and communication: "The paradox, of course, is that Google's intense data collection and number crunching have led it to the same conclusions that good managers have always known. In the best teams, members listen to one another and show sen-sitivity to feelings and needs."[26]

Daniel Goleman observes, "Empathy is particularly important today as a component of leadership for at least three reasons: the increasing use of teams; the rapid pace of globalization; and the growing need to retain talent."[27] For the nonprofit or religious leader who doesn't have the ability to use high salaries as an incentive, who needs to motivate and mobilize volunteers, who is facing the challenges of a rapidly changing post-Christendom world, the capacity to lead others through empathy is even more critical.

Further, empathy is not just a tool that enables us to support, connect, and care for our teammates and followers but also a way to give others courage, lessen anxiety, lower defenses, en-courage collaboration, and move forward with changes that need to be made.

One senior executive of a major manufacturing company told me a story of what happened when the company decided to pay for tools for their workers and no longer require each worker to have their own tools or tool cart. The executives assumed that the employees would love this decision (they would no longer have to spend their own money on their own tools), but they encountered deep resistance. The workers didn't want the company tools; they liked their own tools. No matter how hard the executives tried to explain the rationale (it saved both the individuals and the company money, it increased productivity, it was fairer toward employees who couldn't afford good tools), the employees still resisted giving up their personal tools. Finally, they discovered that there was an even deeper issue that none of the C-Suite leaders expected and that no one talked about in the economic and "rationale" conversation.

One day, the senior executive was walking the floor and one of the workers who was opposing the decision to do away with personal tools asked to talk with him. The executive told me the story.

"He invited me to come over and look at the big tool chest that he kept all his tools in. As I got closer, he said to me, 'Sir, you have an office, right? And you have pictures of your wife and kids in your office?' 'Yes,' I said, 'I like having pictures in my office to remind me of why I work so hard, who I am providing for, and why I want to do a good job every day.' The worker showed me his cart. It was covered with pictures of his family. 'This is my office. If you take away my tools and my tool cart, you are taking away my office.'"

The executive told me that having heard that story, they were still able to make the move they needed to make for the company to pay for and provide tools, but they provided every worker a locker with space for pictures and personal effects to be each person's "office."

In their podcast *The Leaders' Journey*, Jim Herrington and Trisha Taylor define emotional intelligence with four attributes: self-awareness, self-mastery, social awareness, and relationship management. The common threads that weave through these four EQ attributes are being attuned to our own feelings and the feelings of others and allowing that attunement to guide our actions.[28] This emotional attunement, this capacity to listen deeply and *feel with* a person is a skill that again is best developed in the leader in actual work with people. It is developed in conflict, while walking the floor, in a congregational meeting, or even when negotiating with an international terrorist.

For twenty-four years, Chris Voss worked for the FBI, including becoming the International Lead Hostage Negotiator after serving fourteen years as the hostage negotiator for the New York City Joint Terrorist Task Force. For Voss the key to negotiating with terrorists is the same as negotiating a business deal or with an employee (or even, I would add, with a frustrated faculty member or challenging staff member), it's what he calls "tactical empathy."

For Voss, tactical empathy is "understanding the feelings and mindset of another in the moment and also hearing what is behind those feelings so you increase your influence in all the moments that follow."[29] Tactical empathy sounds manipulative, but in truth it is about being completely honest about one's objectives and open to the concerns and needs of other persons. "It's bringing our attention to both the emotional obstacles and the potential pathways to getting an agreement done."[30] It's about the combination of "caring personally" and "challenging directly" that Kim Scott has described in her bestselling book *Radical Candor*.[31] It's attuning to and accompanying people through change.

For the change leader, attunement is not just about caring and convincing but being with people *in such a way that they can face the losses that change will inevitably bring* to them and helping them grow as a result.[32] It's about managing emotionally volatile situations as Jesus did with the woman who was caught in adultery and about to be stoned by a crowd.[33] It's rejoicing with those who rejoice and weeping with those who weep, it is bearing each other's burdens (Romans 12:15; Galatians 6:2) as we go through the change process together.

This requires connection, empathy, courage, and support. When facing our losses and fears, leaders themselves need to find people who attune with them and develop their attunement with others. Leading change requires the capacity to help others *feel accompanied* in the transformational journey as we prepare to make adjustments that will require genuine effort in the face of loss. In other words, attunement is the way we develop and harness the capacity to make major adaptations to our lives, build trust with our followers in the process of working together, and then find the grit to stay with the changes. Upon a grounded identity, and alongside a teachable and attuned character, are two additional characteristics for a resilient change leader: *adaptable* and *tenacious*.

ADAPTABLE

One of the most surprising discoveries in the literature and in conversations with leaders about developing resilience is how important adaptability, creativity, and innovation are for being resilient in the midst of challenges or resistance (see fig. 3.2).

Figure 3.2. Adaptability leads to resilience

For Diane Coutu, who wrote the seminal article on resilience for *Harvard Business Review*, resilience depends on the ability of leaders to face the reality of a situation, find meaning in those challenges and *"make do with whatever is at hand."*[34] Coutu describes this as a kind of "ritualized ingenuity" that takes the core elements of an organization or person's character and combines and adapts them in creative and new ways.

Like the fiery forge that makes the hardened steel malleable, the character of a leader that can "meet the demands of reality" must be up for the task of meeting the demands of a *rapidly changing* reality.[35] That is, it's not enough to stand unwavering for the values and beliefs that have been passed on to us, we must also face the disrupted circumstances that challenge our very understanding of reality and then meet the demands of whatever we discover. Andrew Zolli writes, "In their purest expression, resilient systems . . . *may reconfigure themselves continuously and fluidly to adapt* to ever-changing circumstances, while continuing to fulfill their purpose."[36]

This definition of integrity and this understanding of resilience as requiring adaptability speaks to the kind of tempered quality that is both strong and flexible, both unwavering in the core values and principles that give the person, community, or organization its identity, and then as flexible and malleable as needed to apply those values and principles to a changing, real-world situation. So Paul challenges Peter when he refuses to eat with Gentiles and reverts to the Jewish dietary laws of his pre-conversion days pulling back from table fellowship with Gentile Christians (Galatians 2:11-13). But Paul also acknowledges that when he is in similar enough circumstances, he writes that "to the Jew I became as a Jew" and to the Gentiles he became like them as well to "win" them for Christ (1 Corinthians 9:19-23).

For Paul this is not a chameleon-like changing to blend into a context but a "healthy adaptation of core values" that holds firm to the mission and purpose that is at the center of his identity while being flexible enough in practices to not offend.[37] It gives meaning and purpose to a leader facing opposition and a group that needs to hold on to its reason for changing. Coutu's study shows that resilient leaders find a deep sense of meaning and purpose in the challenges that they are facing. Therefore, she offers, "It should come as no surprise that the most successful organizations and people possess strong value systems. Strong values infuse an environment with meaning because they offer ways to interpret and shape events."[38]

In Jewish and Christian literature the key to *healthy* adaptability is that it remains firmly grounded in one's identity, values, and core commitments. That kind of adaptability overcomes a failure of nerve and resists a failure of heart because of a kind of tensile strength that can withstand the conflict and challenges around them because they have resolved the conflict within them. As Sacks writes, "No one is stronger than the person who knows who and what he is."[39] Resilience requires creativity and innovation to find an adaptive solution amid an intractable problem *without* violating our core beliefs or mission.

> *Once you have decided what will never change, you must be prepared to change everything else.*

When reflection, self-awareness, and vulnerability reinforce integrity and identity, then there is developed a capacity for being adaptable that is often called "agility." One professor of leadership describes it this way:

> Agile leaders are those who so leverage their integrity and identity, that they can then begin to think more creatively and engage in learning as a leader more quickly. "Agile leaders are creative thinkers with a deep sense of purpose. They show a propensity and ability to move into action and make decisions, and their implementation often results in greater learning . . . they 'seek pain to learn.'"[40]

Again, the agility needed for resilience and adaptability is only possible when a person has "bedrock values." Creativity, innovation, risk-taking, the ability to innovate, learn and fail; the capacity to be vulnerable and learn; the aptitude for tolerating the heat of reflection and the exposure of vulnerability is once again dependent on that *grounded* identity.

So, to become resilient depends on the heat of reflection to develop self-awareness and vulnerability that leads to the capacity to take risks and be adaptable. *Adaptability* comes from the *integrity* of character, values, and identity, and serves as an unchanging leverage point for agile, innovative solutions. Once you have decided what will never change, you must be prepared to change everything else.[41]

To *grounded*, *teachable*, *attuned*, and *adaptable*, we now add *tenacious*: what the Scriptures speak of as perseverance or what has become popularly known as *grit* (see fig. 3.3). And this persevering, gritty tenacity is the result of passion and a capacity for perseverance that requires the security found in relationships to grow to fruition.

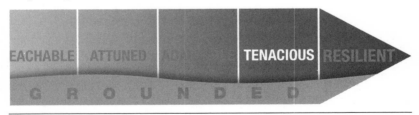

Figure 3.3. Tenacious leaders and the perseverance necessary for resilience

TENACIOUS

Describing what he believed was the most important characteristic of leaders, Edwin Friedman spares no time for subtlety: *"Persistence in the face of resistance and downright rejection,"* he writes (emphasis added).[42]

For Friedman these qualities show up in an almost daunting form of hopeful determination. Persistent leaders, he writes, have "a drive that sometimes may seem to border on the demonic. But no one has ever gone from slavery to freedom with the slaveholders cheering them on, nor contributed significantly to the evolution of our species by working a forty-hour week, nor achieved any significant accomplishment by taking refuge in cynicism."[43] This combination of persistence, drive, and hope is not just some natural toughness that some leaders have and others don't. It is a set of qualities that can be developed and formed in the life of a leader.[44]

For her bestselling book on what makes for success in life, Angela Duckworth studied cadets at West Point, a sales team at a vacation time-share company, students in Chicago Public Schools, and the Green Berets. She also looked at research from others who worked with world-class pianists, neurologists, swimmers, chess players, mathematicians, sculptors, and spelling-bee winners. From that research she concluded that success was not a function of natural talent, education, or social condition as much as the presence of one other factor that is a combination of perseverance and passion:

> The highly successful had a kind of ferocious determination that played out in two ways. First, these exemplars were unusually resilient and hardworking. Second, they knew in a very, very deep way what it was they wanted. They not only had determination, they had direction. It was this combination of passion and perseverance that made high achievers special. In a word, they had grit.[45]

For leaders to face setbacks, they must develop the "grittiness," as Duckworth calls it, to stay with a problem and continue to lead when opposition and resistance are at their highest. If they are leaders, they must be able to communicate hope and keep making decisions that will move the organization toward its goals. They need not only perseverance but passion. Not only a stubborn resolve but a *reason* for being so resolved. The key measure of a gritty person is not staying at something doggedly for hours at a time, nor is it about overworking and driving oneself toward burnout, it's about focusing one's passion and purpose in such a way that you get up again and try again when you fail or are discouraged.[46]

If the first critical element for a leader's development of resilience is self-reflection, then the second, equally critical element is solid, safe relationships.

It's tempting to believe then that resilience and success in life is simply a matter of nose-to-the-grindstone hard work and minimizing social factors and personal challenges that are deeply indicative of a person's success or resilience. (Indeed, Duckworth has been strongly critiqued for seemingly reinforcing this impression).[47] But Duckworth's main point is that grit is one factor of success and that it *can* be developed as a defining aspect of one's character. What Jewish and Christian formation and leadership development literature emphasize is that those factors are most clearly developed in the context of *relationships* with people who share a common, deeply meaningful purpose.

TENACIOUS PASSION

"The heart is both a driving engine and a compass. . . . Grit is thus downstream from longing. People need a powerful why if they are going to be able to endure any how," wrote *New York Times* columnist David Brooks, echoing the words of Nietzsche, that were made famous by Viktor Frankl, psychologist and Holocaust survivor who wrote *Man's Search for Meaning*. [48] Frankl's conviction after seeing both the horrible brutality of the camps and the moments of beautiful, resilient dignity in response by those suffering was to assert:

> There is nothing in the world, I venture to say, that would so effectively help one to survive even the worst conditions as the knowledge that there is a meaning in one's life. There is much wisdom in the words of Nietzsche: "He who has a why to live for can bear almost any how." [49]

We will have much more to think about together in a later section on the *why* of Christian leadership, but for now it's enough to be clear that passion for a task is often linked with a sense of meaning and purpose, and that meaning, purpose, and passion become the fuel of gritty tenacity. "What ripens passion," writes Duckworth, "is the conviction that your work matters. For most people, interest without purpose is nearly impossible to sustain for a lifetime." For Duckworth, grit is not, therefore, a sober-minded, dour, joyless repetition of the necessary "10,000 hours of deliberate practice," but instead the focused hard work of someone who believes that what they are attempting to do really *makes a difference*. [50] "It is therefore imperative that you identify your work as both personally interesting and, at the same time, integrally connected to the well-being of others." [51]

A compelling *why* not only keeps a leader motivated but creates the right combination of the intersection of individual and shared purposes that enables the groups to make agreements, collaborate, and find their "collective genius." One study revealed that high-performing resilient teams don't start with creating trust and developing relationships through activities like corporate retreats with "trust falls" or ropes courses, but instead by focusing on the individual motivations and passions of each person.[52]

When a team cares about the passions of each individual, then it can begin to ask each individual to focus on the collective purpose and goals of the team. This is not always easy. This is usually when conversations between strong-willed, passionate, and capable leaders becomes conflict. But out of these passionate conversations comes a shared sense of purpose, the development of trust, and growth in collective passion. This shared passionate purpose enables the group to stay connected and persevere in the challenge they are facing.

Personal meaning, purpose, and passion are even more powerful when shared by a group who also share a deep and meaningful emotional connection. When David Brooks was teaching a course at Yale and shared a brief moment of vulnerability in class, he was greeted that evening by a dozen or so emails from students who told him that they were praying for *him*. Brooks noted that the rest of the term there was a different quality in the class that came from the connection. "What teachers really teach is themselves—their contagious passion for their subjects and students. . . . Children learn from people they love, and that love in this context means willing the good of another, and offering active care for the whole person."[53]

This is why Silicon Valley executive coach Bill Campbell made his focus with senior leaders at places like Google, Apple, and Intuit the development of teams and building those teams into communities. Google CEO and author of a biography of Campbell, Eric Schmidt, wrote, "Once you have your team or your community, what matters most are the bonds between the people on the team, which are forged by caring *for each other and the common good*."[54]

TENACIOUS PERSEVERANCE

"We rejoice in our sufferings," Paul writes, "knowing that suffering produces endurance, and endurance produces character, and character produces hope" (Romans 5:3-4).

When the Scriptures speak of resilience, the words they most often use are *endurance* and *perseverance*. The Greek word transliterated *hypomone* is used repeatedly to entreat the saints to persevere in faith and faithfulness amid the trials of this world, heaping the highest praise on those who do.[55] The Scriptures are filled with references extolling the "endurance" that comes from testing (James 1:3-4), highlighting the beauty of the "steadfastness of hope" (1 Thessalonians 1:3), and praising those who "overcome" (Revelation 3:5, NKJV) by "enduring patiently" (Revelation 2:3).

Jesus tells a parable about the persistence of a praying widow (Luke 18:1-8) to teach his disciples about what Paul charges his readers, to persevere in prayer for all the saints (Ephesians 6:18). When Martin Luther King Jr. and the leaders of the civil rights movement recruited volunteers to join the movement, they all had to sign a pledge of nonviolence and ongoing prayer for themselves and the movement with "a will to persevere."[56]

Earlier I told the story of our church's capital campaign to rebuild our facilities, the sabotage of church member Jay, and my business administrator's exhortation to consider a "Plan B." Looking back now I realize just how angry and defensive I was, especially at my business administrator. I just wanted my colleague to support our capital campaign and help me get one of our influential donors on board. To be fair, my colleague *was* on my side. His words about looking for an alternative plan were intended to protect the credibility of my pastorate from taking a hit because of a big, expensive, and failed initiative.

But regardless of what my business administrator colleague, Jay, or I were intending, the result of Jay's refusal to support the building campaign and the way he went about it had their good effect on me. They were the crucible for my growth as a leader.

Over the next few months I had to become humbler so that my congregation and my team would be more open to telling me bad news earlier or pointing out missteps (like publicly criticizing previous building campaigns!). I had to ask my leaders to be as candid as possible with information that they assumed I knew (like that Jay built the buildings we were now tearing down). I had to learn to become more attuned to those like Jay who didn't support the campaign but needed to know that even if they didn't agree with me or the direction of the church, this was still their church home and we cared about them. I had to learn to use more empathy than I ever imagined to lead a congregation through an expensive, disruptive, nine-year project, and I had to tenaciously stick to our vision when the 2008 recession put the whole country into an economic tailspin.

The building project, the capital campaign, Jay's sabotage, my colleague's anxiety, and my missteps and miscommunication became the shop for my ongoing leadership formation as a teachable and attuned leader. And like a blacksmith shop there was lots of heat, lots of noise, and lots of opportunities to get hurt. But that is what happens when you enter a place where transformation is happening.

My dad's favorite quote when I was growing up was President Harry Truman's line "If you can't stand the heat, get out of the kitchen." And indeed, that line is apt for leadership in ways that only a president of the United States would know.

But the truth is that the heat of a leadership role is not hot enough *by itself* to bring the transformation that change leaders need. If we are going to become tempered, resilient leaders, we need it to get much, much hotter.

4

HEATING

STRENGTH IS FORGED IN SELF-REFLECTION

*I want to experience your vulnerability but I
don't want to be vulnerable. Vulnerability is
courage in you and inadequacy in me.*

BRENÉ BROWN

*The one who attempts to act and do things
for others or for the world without deepening their
own self-understanding, freedom, integrity and capacity to
love Christ, will not have anything to give others. They will
communicate to others nothing but the contagion of their
own obsessions, their aggressiveness, their ego-centered
ambitions, their delusions about ends and means,
their doctrinaire prejudices and ideas.*

THOMAS MERTON

AFTER THE SAFETY LECTURE and some brief instructions,
our blacksmithing teacher told us to take the prongs, reach
in, and pull out the piece of steel. "Be careful," he said, "it may look
cool, but it's 700 degrees and can burn the skin off your hands."

Cautiously, we novice smiths all held the tongs firmly together and inspected the steel. While I believed my instructor about the temperature and danger (and so did *not* touch it with bare hands), it didn't *look* that different than it had moments before when I plunged it into the forge.

"When a piece of steel looks like this, even coming out of the forge, it's not ready for shaping," he said. "If you hammer on it now, you'll only mar and scar it. And because it doesn't look any different, it's actually more dangerous. If we are going to make this steel into something that can be used, it needs to be much, much hotter—nearly 2,000 degrees. It has to be soft enough and malleable enough to take the shaping. And that requires a lot more heat. So, back into the fire it goes."

BECOMING A TEMPERED LEADER

Working: Leaders are formed in leading.

Heating: Strength is forged in self-reflection.

Holding: Vulnerable leadership requires relational security.

Hammering: Stress makes a leader.

Hewing: Resilience takes practice.

Tempering: Resilience comes through a rhythm of leading and not leading.

If the actual task of leading is the *shop* for forming a leader, the forge that makes the leader ready for the forming is the fire of *vulnerable self-reflection*. If taking on a leadership challenge is to enter the shop and feel the heat of the forge, then allowing the vulnerability of the truth of our weaknesses, insecurities, and need to learn as we go is to like becoming steel that is thrown into the fire.

Imagine yourself in this situation: you are leading a team of people, and your organization is in crisis. Maybe you are running out of money and people fear for their jobs. Maybe you lost a big donor or the attendance at church has been in a yearlong slide. Maybe it's a cultural or global phenomenon like the pandemic of 2020. You are sitting in a meeting and everybody is looking at you. And someone asks, "Well, what do *you* think we should do?"

You feel your face flush and your mouth go dry. Your mind is racing. You desperately want to convey confidence, and you want everyone to trust you. You are so tempted to put on a good face and fake it. And you fear that the next words you need to say are going to change everything.

You take a deep breath and say, "Friends. This is really a hard spot. And here is the honest answer: I don't know what to do."

How does that feel? If you are like me, even thinking about it makes you sick to your stomach. You can even picture the faces of your teammates staring at you in disbelief. You can hear, even in your mind, the muttering.

But if you can stand there and say that, experiencing the vulnerability of that moment, you can begin to develop the strength to lead your group into the transformation that comes in adaptive change.

FORGING FOR LEADING CHANGE

The first step to take while leading through a genuine adaptive challenge is literally to *do* nothing. Don't send an email. Don't call a meeting. Don't read a report. Don't do a "SWOT" analysis.[1] Don't plan. Don't do anything. At least not right away. Resist the temptation to assume that your experience, education, and insight are enough to save the day. The first step for leading through adaptive change is to overcome the impulse to do the first thing or the usual thing that comes to mind in order to project an air of expertise. Resist deploying your "700-degree" self into action and instead turn up and feel the heat through vulnerable self-reflection.[2]

Honest, self-aware, vulnerable, even Spirit-inspired reflection is the critical element that must be present in the life of the leader before the actual shaping, forming, and tempering can begin. In the oft-repeated words attributed to educator John Dewey, "We don't learn from experience, we learn by reflecting on experience."[3]

To enter the forge of leadership is go deeper than entering the shop and taking on the challenges of leading; it is to accept this foundational practice of vulnerable self-reflection as a foundational stance of one's life and leadership functioning: the humbling process of allowing the Spirit, our circumstances, the leadership challenges we face, and especially the failures we experience to grow us in vulnerability and self-awareness. Edwin Friedman wrote that leaders must have a *"willingness* to be exposed and vulnerable." He continues,

> One of the major limitations of imagination's fruits is the fear of standing out. It is more than a fear of criticism. It is . . . a position that puts one's own resources to the test, a position where one will have to take total responsibility for one's own response to the environment. Leaders must not only not be afraid of that position; they must come to love it.[4]

From vulnerability and self-awareness we develop the strength of character that enables us to exercise adaptive leadership and hew hope from despair. Leadership professor and author Dwight Zscheile says, "There is no innovation and learning without vulnerability."[5]

So, the first thing we need to do is *feel the heat* of vulnerability that arises when we reflect and truthfully acknowledge that not only are we *not* the expert with the solution but there may not be an expert present to solve the problem (because if there had been, believe me, we would have solved this problem already). This is not a technical problem that can be solved by the smart application of our expertise but an adaptive challenge that forces the leader to confront the expectations or competing values of the group. Adaptive challenges are the tests of leadership mettle because they force the leader to face the heat of honestly admitting their limitations and saying those words that psychologists tell us are the three hardest words to say: "I don't know."

For someone leading people through change and the learning and loss that is part of the adaptive change process, even admitting that learning is necessary is a kind of loss: loss of esteem, loss of respect, loss of confidence in the eyes of those we are called to lead through change. This alone is a crucible moment that challenges our sense of identity because not only do the people who look to us for those simple answers become disappointed in us, but we tend to feel shameful for not having the answers to give that will satisfy them and make them even more confident in us. A study at the University of Leeds conducted with five-to-eight-year-old children demonstrated that when asked a nonsense question like "What do feet have for breakfast?" or "Is red heavier than yellow?" the majority of kids made up an answer rather than admit that they didn't have one.[6]

The sense of embarrassment for admitting that they didn't have an answer (even to a nonsense question) was too high to risk saying so. But while this may be understandable in a child who is just getting used to answering questions in a classroom, it is the exact opposite of what is needed in a leader. The situation calls for honesty and curiosity that will enable the group to find the right course of action and not default back to whatever they can call to mind or convince others is true in their insecurity. For most leaders, the vulnerability of this moment is overwhelming. It takes great courage because most of us—as followers—are looking for leaders who give us answers. As Ronald Heifetz says, "In a crisis we tend to look for the wrong kind of leadership. We call for someone with answers, decision, strength, and a map of the future, someone who knows where we ought to be going—in short, someone who can make hard problems simple."[7]

THE DANGER AND FUTILITY OF A 700-DEGREE LEADER

The guy at the forge next to mine in the Discovery Class had walked in the door with a burst of enthusiasm. During the safety lecture and the introduction to the class, he interrupted to pepper the instructor with off-topic questions. He'd obviously seen episodes of the History Channel reality show *Forged in Fire*, in which amateur blacksmiths make iconic weaponry, and he was eager to start making anything. Soon he was next to me, hammering away on the little project of the class that day.

But, after about thirty minutes or so, I looked over at him and realized that he had made little progress and was getting frustrated. His steel was mostly just a marred and uneven rod of misshapen metal. And that's when I realized what his problem was: in his enthusiasm, he just kept hammering, even when the steel had cooled below the threshold for forging. The cooling steel resisted shaping. No real formation was coming, and the metal was becoming more filled with stress.

Many of us are like my enthusiastic classmate. We are so eager to be deployed into leadership and to influence others that we neglect this first necessary element for tempering both steel and souls. Either by design or denial we don't spend enough time in the forge, developing the capacity to feel the heat of vulnerable self-reflection that makes us ready for the shaping.

Sometimes we tell stories about how leadership is hard, how we have learned to "stand the heat in the kitchen," and how demanding and vulnerable we are. We sound like we have been through the fire, and we talk like we know the intensity of the forge, but in truth we are only being heated to 700 degrees. Experienced enough to seem tempered for leadership, in reality we are just more dangerous to others and unable to allow the vulnerability of that moment to offer the shaping that we need. So, when the blows come and the hammering of leadership experiences are applied to our lives, we just become more scarred, more stressed, and more misshapen.

Standing in front of people who expect leaders to be unfailing, never-disappointing, and always reassuring experts in the middle of a rapidly disorienting world, and knowing that the truest thing we can say is, "I don't know what to do next," is the moment when leaders have to decide if they are going to go beyond 700 degrees.

And this is also, if we decide not to admit to the moment of vulnerability, when we are most dangerous to ourselves and others. We can tell ourselves that we are ready for this moment, that we know ourselves well and can "fake it until we make it." We can exude confidence that is beyond our competence and get others to follow close behind (even if they may get burned).[8] If being a grounded and teachable leader is critical for the tempered resilience needed to lead change, then the crucibles of leadership are challenges to our identity, and defending against those moments of vulnerability is what makes us dangerous.

The crucible experiences that Warren Bennis and Robert Thomas studied were not formative just because they were hard but because they created "a point of deep self-reflection that forced them to question who they were and what mattered to them. It required them to examine their values, question their assumptions, hone their judgment."[9] Martin Luther King Jr.'s biographer wrote about the sense of doubt that put him into a "daze" as he felt the mantle of responsibility fall on him during the Montgomery bus boycott, which began the civil rights movement;

> *If the actual task of leading is the* shop *for forming a leader, the forge that makes the leader ready for the forming is the fire of* vulnerable *reflection.*

he wondered to himself, "Why has God seen fit to catapult me into such a situation?"[10]

At this moment Dr. King is in deeply biblical company. Moses, who stammered back at God that he couldn't speak well enough to lead; David, Jeremiah, and Josiah were all too young; and Esther was a woman of the wrong nationality to be of any use (or so she thought). In every case, it was the word of God (sometimes through a wise person or prophet of God) that affirmed their call to leadership in this moment of vulnerability. Indeed, Dr. King, honestly facing his doubts about his worthiness as a leader, found the presence of God and strength of call that continued to shape him for his task—especially at those times when he wanted to walk away. Finding himself in a dark night where he "tried to think of a way to move out of the picture without appearing a coward," he turned to God.

> Dropping his head into his hands, he suddenly realized he was praying aloud in the midnight hush of the kitchen: "Lord, I'm down here trying to do what's right. . . . But Lord, I'm faltering, I'm losing my courage. And I can't let the people see me like this. . . . But I've come to the point where I can't face it alone." And at that moment, as King would tell it, he seemed to hear "an inner voice . . . the voice of Jesus," answering him: "Martin Luther, stand up for righteousness, stand up for justice, stand up for truth. And lo, I will be with you, even until the end of the world." That voice of Jesus, King recounted, "promised never to leave me, no, never to leave me alone."[11]

This is just the moment when the leader faces the choice: either turn up the heat by honest self-awareness and vulnerability or stand just close enough to the forge to appear unchanged. The temptation to have it all together, the lure of looking good and safe and respectable is always before us, and it is fueled by both self-doubt and the shame that wants to keep our weaknesses from showing. "Insecurity and defensiveness are what make a poor leader," Lynn Ziegenfuss told me, "because it keeps them from being learners."[12] Note, honest insecurity isn't the problem, the problem is insecurity from defensiveness that turns into pride and keeps the leader from being a *learner*. Humility and teachability show up again and, once again, we become aware that the key to making this moment be even more formative is when a leader deliberately chooses to be a learner.

In 2015, Fuller's Max De Pree Center for Leadership was in trouble. This institute for leadership development that had been named in honor of a great Christian businessperson and author was on life support. As the administration looked for a new executive director, the Center was down to two staff persons and a mostly depleted endowment.

Mark Roberts seemed like just the person to turn things around. Roberts has three earned degrees from Harvard University, including a PhD. He has worked on the staff of one of the most prestigious historic churches in the country, was a senior pastor of another large church for sixteen years, and had been the senior director of Laity Lodge in Texas.

Roberts immediately hit the road to talk to former constituents, pastors, and potential donors to the De Pree Center to see what would be needed to turn the Center around. In listening to dozens of stakeholders, Roberts discovered that the credibility of the Center had been weakened by ineffective programming and unfulfilled promises, and that most leaders weren't interested in either supporting the Center financially or being part of a new season in its life. They wanted to see valuable work being done before they were willing to engage.

With determination, Roberts rolled up his sleeves. If the Center didn't have much, it had him, and he was willing to give his best to it. He continued a pattern that he had begun years before as a pastor and then working for a leadership foundation, of writing an online daily devotional. He took the expertise of his PhD in New Testament and his years of preaching and teaching as a pastor and used that knowledge to serve the people—mostly marketplace leaders—to whom he was listening. The daily devotional, *Life for Leaders* (depree.org/life -for-leaders), started with just a handful of readers, but he could at least have something free to offer people in response to their spending time with him and letting him learn from them what they would want in a leadership center.

Roberts would make plans and try out new ideas. He came up with a plan and pitched it to a foundation to see if they would fund it. They loved the idea so much that they funded it generously—*not* by giving funding to the De Pree Center but to *another organization* they trusted could pull it off because they worried about the Center's unimpressive track record.

Roberts found himself deeply discouraged. "It's one thing to start a new project and ask people to believe in your vision. It's another thing to ask people to believe in your vision for a project that once did good work but became ineffective for several years." He found himself on the verge of despair when he sensed just how bad of shape the Center was in. And within a few weeks another blow hit him, Fuller Seminary, in which the De Pree Center was housed, was facing some significant financial cutbacks. Become financially sustainable in eighteen months, he was told, or the school would have to shut the Center down. Roberts found himself sitting in his backyard morning after morning praying, "Lord, what would you have me do?"

Roberts listened to people and their disappointments in the Center of the past. After a while he began to hear under the criticism the longings and hopes that people had for the Center. He brought those ideas before God and prayed again, "Lord, is this what I am supposed to do?"

Roberts said that he had two firm impressions from God: first, that he was supposed to keep showing up every morning and serving people through writing his devotional and, second, that he was to keep listening to people and learning from them what they need, "what was working, and what was not working." If something worked, they would do more of it, if it didn't work, they would stop the program, learn from the experiment, and move on to the next.

"What I learned in those days was that I really needed to be willing to learn. I needed to learn from the past mistakes; I needed to learn by listening to people in their hopes and dreams; and I needed to learn from my partners and colleagues. I just had to keep being humble before God and being willing to learn as quickly as possible from what wasn't working so we could figure out what would work."[13]

At this writing, over 500,000 times a year somebody chooses to engage with the De Pree Center through their resources and events. They have a strong staff and a solid, growing group of supporters. Roberts discovered in his daily backyard prayers that the more he turned to God to ask what to do, the more God gave him the courage to be willing to listen humbly and experiment, to take the risk of failing, and to be more comfortable with being vulnerable in not having all the answers of exactly what to do. "I had to learn quickly. I had to be willing to learn," he said. Everything began to turn around when a Harvard grad had to *learn to learn* all over again. We will return to the themes of learning and listening again later, but for now I want us to pay deeper attention to what that kind of learning *costs* the leader.

CONSIDER

What does it feel like for *you* to find yourself not as the expert who has the answers but the leader in need of learning?

The kind of vulnerable self-reflection that is necessary for formed, resilient, tempered leaders must be the kind that takes us all the way to "2,000 degrees," to the place where, if we were made of steel, the molecules in the metal begin to change and what was just moments before hard and solid, now literally oozes in a semi-liquid form.

THE OOZY, HUMBLING, OH-SO-VULNERABLE
PROCESS OF BECOMING A LEADER

Becoming tempered leaders requires that we allow ourselves to be thrust into the forge of self-reflection. Self-reflection must lead to self-awareness, and self-awareness—if courageous, honest, and practiced in a place of engaged exposure—leads to feeling vulnerable. And since that vulnerability is a critical asset of a leader, growing in self-awareness is vital to the process of becoming a change leader.

Self-reflection must lead to self-awareness, and self-awareness— if courageous, honest, and practiced in a place of engaged exposure—leads to feeling vulnerable.

Self-awareness is both one of the oft-repeated traits of resilient and creative leaders and also one of the pillars of Ignatian spirituality, a form of Christianity that is practiced by the Society of Jesus. The Society, or the Jesuits as they are most well-known, was founded in the sixteenth century by Ignatius of Loyola and is an order that has had a far-reaching impact around the world, founded some of the most famous universities in the world, and counts Pope Francis among their brethren.[15]

The essence of the Jesuit life and commitment is that it is a missionary order that is not held together by geography and a common shared domestic life but by a shared missional commitment and "spiritual exercises" that each Jesuit commits to practicing as a rule for living. While other orders committed to "stability" as one of the rules of the order, the Jesuits instead committed to go anywhere and do anything for the "greater glory of God." Ignatius of Loyola described that the ideal attitude for a Jesuit was "living with one foot raised" to be ready at a moment's notice to respond to opportunities for making a difference in the world.

Chris Lowney, who trained and lived as a Jesuit before leaving the order to become an executive in corporate business, explains that the foundation for leadership in the life of a Jesuit is a regular, at least once daily, practice of self-reflection. Indeed, for Lowney, "Self-awareness is key to successfully living with one foot raised."[16] Jesuit leaders first *"make their own lifelong commitment to pursue self-awareness. All leadership begins with self-leadership, and self-leadership begins with knowing oneself."*[17]

For the Jesuits this fundamental principle was based on the idea that the exercise of leadership, especially in crucible moments, reveals the true character of a person and that only through self-awareness can we allow those moments of vulnerability to have the effect of opening us up to the deep transformation that leads to resilience for the challenges being faced. Lowney observes, *"Leaders thrive by understanding who they are and what they value, by becoming aware of unhealthy blind spots or weaknesses that can derail them, and by cultivating the habit of continuous self-reflection and learning."*[18]

That self-reflection is not a dispassionate, distanced self-evaluation but a full engagement and honest self-assessment of one's actions, emotions, and motivations. For author and executive coach Jerry Colonna, this is a process of not only reflecting on what we do but a deep understanding of *why* we do it. Colonna calls this "radical self-inquiry" and "the most challenging piece of the [leadership development] formula—indeed, the most important." He defines it "as the process by which self-deception becomes so skillfully and compassionately exposed that no mask can hide us anymore."[19]

Lowering one's mask to oneself and to others is *painfully* vulnerable. Vulnerability, as Brené Brown has spoken and written about so eloquently, is "the emotion that we experience during times of uncertainty, risk, and emotional exposure."[20] It is the courage to "tell the story of who you are with your whole heart" and to show yourself in your imperfections.[21] Vulnerability, in other words, is the feeling that follows self-awareness when we know that our capacities, limitations, emotions, and motivations are exposed and that we are in a position where we very possibly can fail.[22] It's what Roberts felt when talking to one former constituent after another and a foundation turned down funding his idea for the De Pree Center.

Especially those called to leadership of God's people need to allow themselves to experience the exposure of vulnerability. Jesus warns us that everything hidden is eventually exposed (Luke 8:17), and Jonathan Sacks asserts that this kind of honest "rumbling" (as Brené Brown has dubbed it) with God and each other is at the heart of the identity of what it means to be a person and leader of faith.[23] Vulnerability is also the thing that we most admire when we see it in others while most detesting it in ourselves.[24] When Roberts wrestled with God in his early morning prayers, he was a leader living into a deep tradition of Christian leaders who came vulnerably before God.

The reason why the Jewish people are called the "children of Israel" instead of the children of Abraham or the children of Isaac is that both the people and their namesake are known for the honest, vulnerable wrestling with God in the dark of night (Genesis 28:11-17; 32:24-31). "It is at these points of maximal vulnerability that he encounters God and finds the courage to continue despite all the hazards of the Journey."[25] For Sacks, this capacity to come honestly and vulnerably before God, bringing our doubts and fears to God, is what allows a leader to be shaped and tempered as a resilient tool for God's work within God's people and the world.[26]

Four times in the Hebrew Scriptures, Sacks points out, a leader cried out to God asking for death rather than to continue. Moses, Elijah, Jeremiah, and Jonah all prayed a similar prayer. Lincoln and Churchill both suffered from depression. Meriwether Lewis of the famous Corps of Discovery later succumbed to suicide. And Theodore Roosevelt gave his famous "man in the arena" speech that extolled the value of those who "dare greatly" even in failure. For Sacks, this is the mark of the true leader: "To try, to fall, to fear, and yet to keep going: that is what it takes to be a leader. That was Jacob, the man who at the lowest ebbs of his life had his greatest visions of heaven."[27]

To become honest and truly self-aware is to experience the darkness of the night, the heat of the forge, the vulnerability of the fire that seems as if it is melting us down and leaving us as an oozing, molten puddle. It is natural, of course, to want to hide that vulnerability, if not from ourselves than from others. There are times when projecting a calm and confident demeanor is necessary to keep the trust of an anxious or doubting people. But if the leader must continually project solidity that they don't feel, there is a tragic—and potentially soul-destroying—missed opportunity.

> *To try, to fall, to fear, and yet to keep going: that is what it takes to be a leader. That was Jacob, the man who at the lowest ebbs of his life had his greatest visions of heaven.*

If we never risk bringing our most vulnerable and self-aware souls to the God who is truly able to hold us and shape us through it, then we remain 700-degree leaders, and neither we nor our people are formed. Only in vulnerability are whole-hearted engagement, connection, and trust formed between a leader and a people. It requires demonstrating courage at the very place that we feel most afraid; it is acknowledging that we can't wait to be in safe and trusted relationships to be vulnerable, that vulnerability is a "slow-building, iterative, and layered" process that happens over time. Both trust-building and rum-bling with vulnerability involve risk that requires us[28]—in the inelegant phrase of Brené Brown—to "embrace the suck."[29]

Because we are not trained for this exposure, we understandably—and unfortunately—defend ourselves against the malleability caused by the forge, and we take the blows of leading in a cool and detached posture. We take on more stress without shaping, and we don't invite the people into the process of transformation. Soon protecting oneself leads to danger and defensive cynicism that Jimmy Mellado, the president and CEO of Compassion International, calls "endemic and soul-fracturing. . . . The single biggest issue in the non-profit world is that you end up doing God's work in a way that destroys God's work in you."[30] The result is that people remain fragile and the leaders become brittle.

LEADERSHIP HARDENS THE LEADER

We will continually come back to the blacksmithing paradox that is also present when we are in the middle of a leadership challenge. *Hammering adds stress that brings strength.* Whether the tool is being used (hammering) or shaped (hammered on) the steel takes the stress of the hammering into itself. For the leader, on one hand, the very stress that is applied is the cru-cible that is creating the strength and toughness that we need to be hammered into us. On the other hand, too much pounding either on the tool or with the tool puts so much stress into the steel that it becomes brittle. No one knows when the next blow will blow the chisel apart.

Usually, the signs of this overstressed and therefore danger-ously fragile leader look remarkably like the wizened experi-enced leader who has been in the trenches for years. And it's easy to assume that because we have been in these situations and have performed well that we are up for and able to contend with the next rock of resistance that needs to be removed.

It's also easy to assume that if the goal is to break through the mountain of despair, then there is nothing better for the job than the tested steel of a tough, experienced, chiseled leader. But remembering the wording of Dr. King's speech on the footsteps of the Lincoln Memorial, we realize the goal is not to break *down* or break *through* resistance but to *transform* it. It is to hew stones of hope, to transform discord into "broth-erhood." This transformation requires more than just hardness and strength; it requires the strength and flexibility of being tempered. It requires more than just hammering; it requires an ongoing process of heating, holding, hammering, and tem-pering. It requires that we become more than hard if we are to avoid becoming brittle and are able to continue to lead and serve amid opposition, fear, and resistance. For Jesuit-trained Chris Lowney, the more challenging the context, the more it calls for learning and self-reflection.

> As the world becomes even more complex and changes even faster than Loyola's topsy-turvy sixteenth-century environment, it becomes increasingly clear that only those with a deeply in-grained capacity for continuous learning and self-reflection stand a chance of surfing the waves of change successfully.[31]

Drawing on the metaphor from his professional field, medicine, Heifetz reminds us that leadership first requires diagnosis (or an honest self-assessment) and then action. What is critical for the leader is that those two processes are focused on both the organizational and social systems that we are leading and on our own self.

> To lead effectively, you also have to examine and take action toward yourself in the context of the challenge. In the midst of action, you have to be able to reflect on your own attitudes and behavior to better calibrate your interventions into the complex dynamics of organizations and communities. You need perspective on yourself as well as on the systemic context in which you operate.[32]

Reflection leads to self-awareness that is experienced as vulnerability, but in leading it shows up as *discernment and effectiveness amid change.* And this is the unexpected insight: Because it builds capacity for vulnerability, reflection is what enables the leader to be adaptable, and *adaptable leaders are more resilient leaders.* (Which is a component of the tempered resilience leader that we will examine a bit later.)

> *Because it builds capacity for vulnerability, reflection is what enables the leader to be adaptable, and adaptable leaders are more resilient leaders.*

So, if this kind of resilient adaptability is dependent on the heat of reflection, self-awareness, and vulnerability, what then can we do to become more reflective leaders? How do we begin to take steps to allow ourselves to be placed into the forge and let reflection lead us to self-awareness, vulnerability, and adaptability? Let me tell you where *not* to start and then I'll give the first step.

Brené Brown warns that "vulnerability minus boundaries is not vulnerability. . . . Vulnerability is a slow stacking over time of vulnerability and trust."[33] So, do *not* start being completely vulnerable, showing up in the courage of your whole self in your next staff meeting, board meeting, or meeting with your supervisor. Do not walk into a room and start "rumbling" with colleagues about your sense of insecurity, your blind spots, and your doubts.

Most organizations are not designed for this kind of heat. It would be like setting a fire to do some blacksmithing on the Communion table of a church. There is a reason why blacksmiths use forges. There needs to be safe ways to contain and focus the heat until the organizational trust matches the capacity for vulnerability. And especially for some, the risk of vulnerability is far too high.

For younger leaders, newer leaders, women, and leaders of color, this kind of vulnerability in the wrong context quickly becomes an excuse for the organization to double down on the old model of aged (usually white) males who are assumed to be "expert" leaders that reinforces the status quo and technical competence.

There is a reason why blacksmiths use forges. There needs to be safe ways to contain and focus the heat until the organizational trust matches the capacity for vulnerability.

A woman who has been the senior pastor of a large, multi-staff congregation in New York City for over twenty years told me, "It took sixteen years before I could be this vulnerable with my colleagues or the board. For far too long somebody was lurking around the corner just waiting for me to make a mistake or show a weakness that they could use as an excuse to remove a woman from leadership." Similarly, I heard an African American scholar who is now a vice president in a graduate school say at a lecture, "As a woman of color, I have always had to prove myself in the face of a bias of 'assumed incompetence.' Until I demonstrated my competence a number of times, the assumption was that I was *not* competent—often for years after I was serving ably in the role."

This is a bind. You have to practice being vulnerable to be a leader, and the very act of leadership often works against that necessary vulnerability. Reflection and vulnerability *for* leading (self-awareness) must precede vulnerability *in* leading (adaptability). But even if we can't *publicly* say "I don't know," we begin to become tempered if we can admit it to ourselves and to trusted friends or advisers.

Let's be clear, being that vulnerable while leading *is exactly what is needed* to become a tempered and resilient leader, and to the degree that we have the authority and trust to create the safe spaces to be this vulnerable, we need to. This is the essence of oozy, reflective, vulnerable leadership. This is the heat that transforms. But, like the beginning discovery class that my wife and I took to learn blacksmithing, we all need safe places to learn to experience the heat of reflection, self-awareness, and vulnerability that develops adaptability.

And one great place to begin doing that is with an old prayer at a dinner with people we love and trust.

PRAYER OF EXAMEN AND SUNDAY DINNERS

In the wake of the 9/11 attacks on the Pentagon and the World Trade Center, my wife came up with a plan that changed our family forever. I was readying myself for work in what was still the early morning in California when the first plane hit the first

World Trade Center tower. My wife came into our bedroom and dragged me to the television, and we watched the video of the horror as it was replayed over and over again. Soon the second plane hit the second tower, and now we knew that this was not some freakish accident but an act of terrorism.

I drove the mile to the church building where I was pastoring. We had to notify preschool parents and have them pick up their children. We began to make plans for how we would respond pastorally to the national tragedy, and by that evening, without anything more than emails, a phone chain, and neighborly word of mouth (this was before social media of any kind), we had a packed sanctuary of prayerful, fearful, and anxious people seeking God's comfort, protection, and understanding.

For my Presbyterian congregation in San Clemente, California, that sense of immediacy was even more acute. The Camp Pendleton Marine base that was two miles from our church was on lockdown and high alert. We were told that the San Onofre Nuclear Generating Station that was 2.5 miles from our church was on a list of possible next targets that needed protecting. For a town that had annual drills with air-raid sirens to prepare for a possible nuclear reactor leak, the tension was particularly high.

Within days, my wife, Beth, proposed that we begin what would become an enduring family tradition. I remember her saying, "We don't know what the future holds. We don't know if there will be another attack or if we will be personally touched by it all. We can't live in fear, and I am concerned that we will lose track of how all of this is affecting us. So, I want us to start a family tradition that will keep us, no matter what, connected and checking in with each other. I want us to stay connected at a deeper level and remain grateful for everything we have."

So she laid out the ground rules: "Every Sunday night we will have Sunday dinner together.

"After you get up from your post-preaching nap, no more working.

"The kids will come home from playing with friends, and there will be no more school work either. We'll all gather together and cook a big family dinner.

"We'll have dessert (even when we are on 'diets,' because Sunday is a liturgical feast day).

"We'll light candles and say the Lord's Prayer, and then we'll check in with each other and talk. No media, no rushing. A long, slow family dinner."

We introduced our two children to something we called "Holy High-Low," where each person has to say one high point of the week and one low point. Our children were eight and four at the time, but we wanted them to learn to be reflective. As a family we wanted to become comfortable both thinking intentionally and then sharing the rumblings of our hearts in both joy and anxiety. Over the years, as the children grew, we helped them see that what we were doing was a version of the Ignatian prayer of examen (sometimes called the prayer of awareness).[34]

The prayer of examen is a regular prayer of reflection in the Jesuit tradition where in gratitude for the day we call to mind the moments of strongest feelings or experiences that seem to linger and have left an impression on us. Ignatius called these "interior movements," and he believed that by paying attention to them with increasing self-awareness we could grow closer to God and more aligned with his will.

After calling to mind those moments, we ask ourselves two questions. Were those feelings "consolations" or "desolations," that is, did those interior movements and experiences bring us closer to God or lead us away from God? Jesuit priest and author Kevin O'Brien describes the two movements:

> Did they draw you closer to God? Did they help you grow in faith, hope, and love? Did they make you more generous with your time and talent? Did they make you feel more alive, whole, and human? Did they lead you to feel more connected to others or challenge you to life-giving growth?
>
> Or did the feelings lead you away from God, make you less faithful, hopeful, and loving? Did they cause you to become more self-centered or anxious? Did they lure you into doubt and confusion? Did they lead to the breakdown of relationships?[35]

The prayer of examen helps us to see God's presence through the discipline of regular, honest reflection on the actual events of the day. For the change leader amid the challenge of resistance, to cultivate an awareness of God's presence, gratitude for small gifts of the day, and the vulnerability to come honestly before God in self-awareness is a core practice for developing discernment, adaptability, and courage.

Perhaps the most important aspect of the prayer of examen for our family was to spend years in a regular conversation about the "interior movements" of our souls, the presence of God, and the leading of the Spirit in those movements. Over the years those conversations with our children became the place where we discussed the biggest decisions we made as a family, and they developed the practice of learning how to be reflective, self-aware, and vulnerable with each other.

To be sure, the prayer of examen can and often is practiced alone.[36] But the great gift of years of family dinners and Holy High-Low was the amount of trust we developed with each other. Today, my young-adult children, who both live some distance from us, lead "family dinners" with their local friends and are committed to building community, trust, and resilience for thriving in a changing world. Whenever they are home, we have a family dinner and engage in the long, slow conversation that was shaped by years of dinners and prayers of examen.

And as a leader, that combination of the power of self-reflection and the strength of relationships has helped me to see that every forge is paired with an anvil, that the heated steel needs something solid to hold it.

It is to the leader's anvil that we turn next.

5

HOLDING

VULNERABLE LEADERSHIP REQUIRES RELATIONAL SECURITY

Lay me on an anvil, O God.
Beat me and hammer me into a crowbar.
Let me pry loose old walls.
Let me lift and loosen old foundations.

Prayers of Steel, Carl Sandburg

Each one helps the other,
saying to one another, "Take courage!"
The artisan encourages the goldsmith,
and the one who smooths with the hammer
encourages the one who strikes the anvil,
saying of the soldering, "It is good."

Isaiah 41:6-7

A GLANCE INTO THE OPENING OF THE FORGE revealed an inferno of blazing fire and metal. The heatwaves created a gauzy view; the edges of the steel amid the fire blurred. In this state, now somewhere between 1,500 and 2,000 degrees, there were no exact lines between the edge of the steel and the fire that surrounded it. All was a bright, fiery glow.

"Okay, reach in with your tongs and pull out the steel. Notice the color." The glowing reds, yellows, oranges, and white pulsated the air.

"Put it immediately on the anvil. Don't wave it around. Don't carry it through the shop. Don't try to do anything to it until it is on the anvil. The only safe place for something that hot is on an anvil."

So, the moment of high heat, when the hammering process is going to begin, is when the shaping of the steel is most necessary—and most magical. But that magical moment is dependent on the most earthbound of items. That elixir-like molten steel is placed on a solid foundation. *Heating requires holding.*

BECOMING A TEMPERED LEADER

Working: Leaders are formed in leading.

Heating: Strength is forged in self-reflection.

Holding: Vulnerable leadership requires relational security.

Hammering: Stress makes a leader.

Hewing: Resilience takes practice.

Tempering: Resilience comes through a rhythm of leading and not leading.

In the same way that it is impossible to form raw steel without fire, it is impossible to shape that molten steel without an anvil. Indeed, it is dangerous to do so. Likewise in the formation of a tempered, resilient leader.

If the first critical element for a leader's development of resilience is vulnerable self-reflection, then the second, equally critical element is solid, safe relationships. Thick, heavy relationships. If vulnerable self-reflection that comes during a leadership challenge is like a fire, then relationships are like an anvil that can hold us in our most vulnerable, malleable, and oozy moments in life and leadership—and keep us and those around us safe.

If the first critical element for a leader's development of resilience is vulnerable self-reflection, then the second, equally critical element is solid, safe relationships. Thick, heavy relationships.

WHEN THE WHOLE CHURCH WALKS OUT

When Kevass Harding was appointed pastor of Dellrose United Methodist Church in Wichita, Kansas, it was a homecoming for him. The former college football standout who had been offered a tryout with the Kansas City Chiefs had also served as a police officer for three years in the very neighborhood that was now going to be his parish. A neighboring church to one of the largest United Methodist African American churches and the place where Harding had been trained as an associate pastor, Dellrose was mostly white, mostly aging, and declining when Harding started his appointment in August 1998.

When he arrived as pastor, the church membership that had once been over five hundred people was down to 131, with about half of that in regular worship attendance. While the church was declining, the neighborhood was growing. It had just changed from mostly white to mostly African American, and it was with a hope that an African American pastor trained at a megachurch a mile away could bring with him the prescription that would help this shrinking congregation change the way it ministered to the changing residents of the community.

Harding turned, as he had been trained, to the United Methodist Book of Discipline that charges a pastor and a congregation to "make every effort" to "alter its programs to meet the needs and cultural patterns of the new residents." This meant that the church, which was still functioning with the ministries and patterns of a predominantly white congregation from their 1970s heyday, had some serious changes to make. They assured him in the interview process that they were eager to do so and for him to lead them. But, as Harding writes in his book, *Can These Bones Live?*, "I soon discovered that when some people talk about transition that is all it is—talk!"[1]

Within six months, all but twenty-five members had left.

Two different initiatives to try to have Harding removed as the pastor had been attempted during those months, and as 1999 began, the church and the pastor were in a moment of deep crisis. Recalling these events twenty years later, Harding said,

> I call that time, "The Exodus." It was so painful, that I just about quit the ministry. I felt like I was tricked. I was told when I came that I was to reach the community, but what they wanted was for the new people who came to accommodate the old guard. They wanted me to make the neighborhood people comfortable in a church that didn't want to change to welcome them or accommodate them.
>
> Soon, I was reaching out to people in the neighborhood and when they actually started coming, the people in the church became enraged. Members of the church were *angry* because we were bringing in neighborhood kids.
>
> I knew there was racism, but the one place where I thought it wouldn't be was in the church. I was 30 years old. I was going to lead a church that was going to make a difference. And I got smacked in the face with racism. Even today it brings tears.[2]

Not only did Harding survive those disappointing years, but he led Dellrose United Methodist Church to a new day. At this writing it is a congregation of over eight hundred members and is a thriving part of the neighborhood. But when I asked him how he survived those hard days of the exodus, he answered with two words: *My wife.*

A football player by training and a believer in teamwork and team approaches to ministry, Harding admits that while he teaches the Jethro-Moses-Aaron-Miriam model of shared ministry, he didn't ask for as much help as he could have back then. Leading the church took its toll on him. There were many days of deep discouragement and even despair, but the connection, support from, and partnership with his wife, Teketa, was the difference-maker. "You need a strong support system, and she was mine. I would want to quit, and she would tell me, 'God didn't bring you this far to quit now.' So, I just kept going."

Keep going. These words, whispered at the right time, are more powerful than we know for helping a leader find the resilience when resistance is at its peak. In a book about lessons on perseverance that comes from his Lakota grandfather, Joseph M. Marshall strikes a similar note to the words of Harding's wife.

> Grandfather says this: "Life can give you strength. Strength can come from facing the storms of life, from knowing loss, feeling sadness and heartache, from falling into the depths of grief. You must stand up in the storm. You must face the wind and the cold and the darkness. When the storm blows hard you must stand firm, for it is not trying to knock you down, it is really trying to teach you to be strong.... Grandfather says: Keep going."[3]

In the leadership literature on resilience, the most important words, however, as powerful as they are, are not the words *keep going* but *Grandfather says*. What often gets overlooked in popular resilience books is how often resilience is a result of *relationships*. As Duke Divinity School professor C. Kavin Rowe says, "We often think of resilience in individual terms: this or that person is resilient. But . . . start talking with resilient leaders and soon enough you will see that someone hoped for them in a time when they couldn't get back up. Resilience, in this understanding, is a communal practice, the fruit of a common life rooted in hope itself."[4]

In my own life and leadership, I have experienced that my worst times as a leader are not when things are going wrong but when I feel like I am facing the challenges and resistance alone. When my voice feels like it is echoing off of closed ears and hard hearts, when I think my best ideas are not being considered, that I am being marginalized by other organizational agendas or that the team stops functioning—for whatever reason—as a team.

I have had those experiences when I was the most senior leader on the team and when I was a supporting cast member for another more senior leader. The hardest moments are not when we are facing a challenge but when the alliance—even momentarily—falls apart. (On the flip side, I was asked once in an interview what my greatest joy in leadership is. I knew immediately, "Having a big task—that might fail—that I get to take on with a great team." Big task. Some risk. Great team. That is joy.)

When resilient leaders are interviewed about how they bounced back, they inevitably respond by name-dropping. Whether it is Kevass Harding, Mark Roberts, or the number of young adults who stayed in school when others around them were dropping out, there is a common refrain, "My grandmother was there," "there was a coach," "a youth pastor took me under her wing." In a study of at-risk teenagers and young adults who didn't drop out of high school or who returned to graduate after dropping out, the most significant variable was a significant relationship with someone who encouraged them and believed in them. The study concludes, "Young people are more likely to graduate if they have access to an anchoring relationship and a web of supportive relationships." Notice that it is both *one* anchoring person *and* a web of support. Resilience, especially the capacity to face setbacks and resume working toward the goal of graduating, required a heavy anvil of multiple relationships.[5]

> *What often gets overlooked in discussions of grit and perseverance is how pervasively important is the power of relationships to help us develop tenacity.*

Perseverance not only enables us to develop tenacity but also inspires others to persevere *with us*. Acts of resilience and perseverance remind us that we can't outgrit the challenges we face by ourselves. The Navy SEALs go through "hell week" not only to weed out the weak but to teach the strong that they will only endure if they learn to rely on each other.[6] Charles Duhigg writes in *The Power of Habit* that one of the most important ways to persevere in a change process is having a peer group that is changing *with* you to keep you inspired. This is why people who join an exercise *group* are more likely to stick with an exercise plan than those who work out alone.

Even more, for *leadership* resilience a *relational* approach to forming tenacity is important.[7] In recent discussions about resilience in senior leadership, there is an agreement that senior leaders must focus simultaneously on developing the kind of tenacity internally (*intra*personal), in relationships (*inter*personal) and within the group, team, company or institution (*organizational*).[8]

Similarly, Sacks's commentary on the significance of the role of Moses' sister Miriam as support for Moses while leading the people of God through the wilderness harkens back to the counsel of Moses' father-in-law Yitro (Jethro), in Exodus 18. Note the layers of relationships needed in the life of a leader:

> It is a cliché to say that leadership is a lonely undertaking. But at the same time no leader can truly survive on his or her own. Yitro told Moses this many years earlier. Seeing him leading the people alone he said, "You and these people who come to you will only wear yourselves out. The work is too heavy for you; you cannot handle it alone" (Ex. 18:18). Leaders need three kinds of support: (1) allies who will fight alongside them, (2) troops or teams to whom they can delegate, and (3) a soulmate or soulmates to whom they can confide their doubts and fears, who will listen without an agenda other than being a supportive presence, and who will give them the courage, confidence, and sheer resilience to carry on.[9]

In one study after another of those leaders who have resilience, grit, perseverance, or tenacity, it cannot be overstated how strongly the connection is between resilience and relationships. The qualities that make a tenacious, tempered, resilient leader are—from start to finish—developed relationally. Over and over again at the moments when the leadership challenges are the toughest and the forge of reflection creates self-awareness and vulnerability, the anvil of relationships helps the leader recover the passion and the perseverance necessary to continue to lead change.

There is another, equally critical, factor for success in companies: teams that act as communities, integrating interests and putting aside differences to be individually and collectively obsessed with what's good for the company. Research shows that when people feel like they are part of a supportive community at work, they are more engaged with their jobs and more productive. *Conversely, a lack of community is a leading factor in job burnout.*[10]

Which takes us back to the role of the anvil.

Leaders who seek to bring change and to allow themselves to experience the vulnerability and self-awareness from a life of honest self-reflection need more relationships, not fewer. They need a "thick, heavy" anvil of a host of relationships: partners, colleagues, allies, friends, family, and, perhaps most importantly, mentors. The more daunting the leadership task, the more heat is generated that leaves the leader feeling exposed and oozy, the thicker the anvil must be.

For Mark Roberts, sitting in his backyard, asking God to give him vision and direction for the De Pree Center when there were few donors, a bare-bones staff, little interest from potential clients, a history with a bad organizational track record, and an institution focused on cutting costs, his faithfulness in writing *Life for Leaders*, his life of prayer, and his determination to find a way forward for the Center was made resilient through several relationships. As Roberts tells it, it is clear that he believes he needed them all. Like Kevass Harding, the first relationship Roberts mentions is his wife, Linda. But then he adds, "I had one colleague that I could confide in. But I also had friends and a great spiritual director. Without them," his voice trails off, "I don't know . . ."[11]

Roberts points to what the University of Notre Dame business and management professor Matt Bloom discovered in his work with ministry and nonprofit leaders. Resilience requires leaders to have supportive relationships in different *roles*. Taking a page from Erving Goffman's dramaturgical perspective of social interaction, Bloom writes that to flourish in ministry or other forms of social leadership, leaders need to be conscious of at least three different contexts, and the relationships needed to flourish in those contexts: "front stage, backstage, and offstage."[12] According to Bloom, "The front stage is where performance happens. The backstage is the place to support and nurture great front-stage performances. And the off-stage is a place to step away from performance roles and engage other parts of life."[13]

> *The qualities that make a tenacious, tempered, resilient leader are—from start to finish—developed relationally.*

It's a tragic irony that while so many leaders are expected to maintain relationships and work with numerous constituents, many leaders report being lonely and feeling isolated in their leadership role. From numerous conversations I have had over the years, it's apparent that too many leaders have too few relationships in too few different parts of their lives. When I coach leaders, I encourage them to have the heaviest, thickest anvil possible by considering the different kinds of relationships needed for the demands of leading change.

LEADING ON THE FRONT STAGE

The *front stage* is the place where the actual work of leading a group of people toward a shared transformational goal occurs. Front stage relationships are peers and teammates, our partners and colleagues. Like a cast of actors who brave the gaze of an audience to perform, or like the blacksmiths of the city square in Prague plying their craft to a crowd, the front stage is where leaders are expected to demonstrate their leadership prowess. Bloom's research shows that critical to resilience for ministry leaders is the experience of having trustworthy colleagues joining them in the work and allowing leaders to "be themselves." They then lead from within their own grounded identity and enjoy the camaraderie of allies and teammates who share a common goal.

When asked in an interview about the importance of relationships for a leader, Ronald Heifetz responded, "I live in Boston. No one would live in Boston without owning a winter coat. But countless people think that they can exercise leadership without partners or without a sanctuary."[14] Note how *partners* for leaders are considered essential equipment.

In *Canoeing the Mountains* I wrote extensively about the six different relationships that are identified by Heifetz, Linsky, and Grashow that every leader has to manage.[15] Of those six relationships (allies, confidants, opponents, dissenters, senior authorities, and casualties) all but one (confidants) are frontstage or backstage relationships. But by far the most important for building the relational security of a heavy anvil amid leading change are *allies*.

Allies are not necessarily our friends but our partners. They are people within the organization who are committed to the same transformation even if they have other (even competing) loyalties. As a leader they offer perspective and connection to other potential allies.[16] They are so critical to our ability to lead change that Heifetz and colleagues assert that identifying allies is necessary *prework* that must be undertaken *before* a change process can begin. "Before you go public with your initiative (whether through making a big announcement or simply raising the subject at a meeting), you need to line up enough support to keep your intervention (and you) alive once the action starts."[17]

Moses' brother, Aaron, becomes his first ally in leading the people of God to freedom. Martin Luther King Jr. was part of an alliance of leaders who were drawn together during the Montgomery Bus Boycott long before he became their designated spokesperson.

Management consultant Margaret Wheatley says the quality of relationships, the sense of being known, and the depth of trust in each other in front-stage relationships is not just so a team functions well, but it's also the way a group prepares for the future. In an article on leading during uncertain times, she writes,

> The primary way to prepare for the unknown is to attend to the quality of our relationships, to how well we know and trust one another. . . . There is one core principle for developing these relationships. People must be engaged in meaningful work together if they are to transcend individual concerns and develop new capacities.[18]

Notice that for Wheatley these are specifically front-stage relationships. Organizational trust for bringing change is not built during happy hour or social engagements outside of work. Trust for facing the unknown is built on the stage, or returning to blacksmithing, in the shop where the forges are blazing, the hammers are flying, and tools are being formed and tempered, being made ready for use.

LEARNING IN THE BACKSTAGE

Good front-stage work, however, depends on lots of time backstage analyzing and thinking about the work that is being done, learning from the lessons of both successful and failed leadership initiatives, and especially gaining perspective from experienced leaders. Backstage relationships are the supervisors, mentors, and coaches who help you lead even better when you step on to the front stage again.

In multiple studies and in Jewish and Christian literature, the role of an elder counselor, a wise mentor, or an engaged teacher is extolled as critical for leadership development and success. Moses' father-in-law is the exemplar mentor offering wise advice for managing the demands of leading the people of God (Exodus 18). Barnabas is a sponsor and mentor for the young convert Saul of Tarsus who would become Paul the apostle and later another mentor for John Mark when he fails Paul on a missionary journey.

Unfortunately, much of the actual evidence is that coaching and mentoring adults is far less fruitful than we would hope. In a collaboration with the Murdock Trust, Lynn Ziegenfuss, then vice president of leadership development for Youth for Christ/USA, Walter Wright, the former president of Regent College, and their faculty team discovered the reasons why so many adult mentoring programs flounder when the reputation of youth mentoring programs (like Big Brother, Big Sister; Boys and Girls Clubs; Young Life; Youth For Christ, etc.) are so highly valued and successful. Ziegenfuss and Wright concluded that there is a critical difference in successful youth and adult mentoring.

While youth mentoring success is largely based on the energy, initiative, and commitment of the mentor in the mentoring relationship, adult mentoring success is almost entirely dependent on the energy, initiative, and ownership of the relationship by the *mentee* (or what Wright calls mentorees).[19]

> Mentoring is a relationship shaped by mentorees who accept responsibility for their own development. . . . The mentoree's learning needs define where mentoring is desired, and mentoring relationships intentionally focus on the mentoree's developing vision, values, perspective, knowledge, or skills. It is voluntary; mentorees choose mentors to guide them along a particular portion of their journey.[20]

Wright and Ziegenfuss are highlighting that the backstage is the place where most leaders have to intentionally choose to allow their vulnerable, malleable, oozy, 2,000-degree self to be seen, held, and coached by trusted advisers. And this is rarer than we would think.

LEARNING FROM PSYCHOLOGISTS AND MOB BOSSES

The groundbreaking television show *The Sopranos* was notable for the plotline that Mafia mob boss Tony Soprano was suffering from panic attacks and had decided to enter psychotherapy. One story line from the show is that the therapist herself was also in supervision where she could talk candidly and confidentially about the challenges of trying to do psychotherapy with a man who was begrudgingly talking about the panic attacks, his kids, his marriage, and his mother and was also committed to a life of racketeering, extortion, and murder. Very often both the client and therapist and the therapist and her supervisor struggled in different appointments to figure out the best course of action for a psychologist who was treating a mob boss. While there was lots of support, empathy, and understanding to build trust in the professional relationships, the therapist often confronted the mob boss about whether he was truly willing to change, and likewise the supervisor often challenged the therapist about her motives for being willing to see a man who seemed more committed to a life of sociopathic crime than any true change and growth. But, and this is what made the drama that made for such a compelling show, both the client and his therapist, and the therapist and her supervisor, were deeply engaged in vulnerable conversations.

For years my wife, Beth, had a practice as a marriage and family therapist. For a few of those years she served on a task force for our presbytery (the local district of Presbyterian churches to which our congregation and I, as its pastor, were accountable) addressing sexual misconduct issues between clergy and congregants or clergy and staff. She also served as a consultant when pastors and

> *The absurd expectation that a leader doesn't need anyone else to lead well is one of the greatest problems of the mental models of leadership.*

their Sessions ended up in too much conflict to handle for themselves. In other words, my wife—herself a pastor's wife—saw the very worst sides of pastors and the pain that they caused.

One day she came home from a particularly hard meeting and in exasperation said aloud, "Why don't you pastors all have a supervisor? Why don't you have someone you can talk to when you are at a vulnerable crossroad and are prone to making mistakes? As a therapist there is a professional expectation and responsibility that if we are seeing clients, we will have a supervisor. Tod, I have fifteen clients, and the state of California expects me to seek counsel for serving them well. You have fifteen hundred members in your church and you don't have to talk to anyone!"

What *The Sopranos* raised and what Beth was pointing out is *the absurd expectation that a leader doesn't need anyone else to lead well—one of the greatest problems of the mental models of leadership.* Indeed, many consider it a sign of weakness when a leader not only doesn't know what to do but needs to ask for help (including Tony Soprano's fellow mobsters, by the way, so he tried to keep his therapy secret).

As Sacks points out, to lead alone is not only absurd but is described in the Scriptures in the harshest of terms. When Moses' father-in-law arrives to visit and finds him leading alone:

> He says, "What you are doing is not good" (Ex. 18:17). This is one of only two instances in the whole Torah in which the words lo tov, "not good," appear. The other is in Genesis (2:18), where God says, "It is not good [lo tov] for man to be alone." We cannot lead alone. We cannot live alone. To be alone is not good.[21]

LETTING DOWN OFFSTAGE

When I was nineteen, the youth organization I worked in held its national convention at the Disneyland Hotel. The conference organizers arranged with Disneyland to have a surprise appearance by Mickey Mouse. One of the conditions of having the famous Disney mascot was that Mickey needed a bodyguard, not an actual armed security officer but someone who would stay with Mickey offstage and make sure that no one bothered him—or even saw him.

I was that bodyguard. I was the only person allowed in the offstage room where Mickey rested and waited for his cue to go on. I had to make sure that no one saw Mickey, that no one took any pictures, and that no one even knew so as not to ruin the surprise. But when we were waiting for Mickey to go on, *she* took off her costume head and smoked a cigarette.

Mickey Mouse on stage was a beloved mythical cartoon character loved by generations. Offstage, Mickey was a shy, kind five-foot-tall petite woman whose name I never got. I often imagine that when the actress who plays Mickey Mouse goes home every day that she is probably both exhilarated at the joy she brings to others and relieved to be herself for a while. Her friends may know what she does for a living, but if they are good friends, they won't need her to be Mickey, just herself. Resilient leaders need to have these same offstage relationships too.

For years when I was a pastor in San Clemente, I had one good friend who was about a dozen years older than me. He was raising teenagers when I had toddlers; he was paying for weddings for his five kids when I was paying for braces and sports activities for my two. We would often walk the ridge trail in our town, and I would listen to any advice he would generously and gently offer. He and his family were deeply involved in the church, but it was clear that our friendship mattered more to him than whether I was his pastor. When the time came for me to discern whether I should be open to an invitation to leave the church and join the administration of Fuller Seminary, he was the first person in the congregation who I asked for advice.

Looking back, I realized that as often as I had wanted him to be in some form of official leadership for the church, he had always declined. At the time I was disappointed. He was a successful businessman, he was deeply trusted in the community, and his life was marked by winsomeness and wisdom. He would have made a great church leader. But he was more committed to me personally than to the shared work we had at the church. And the gift of his friendship endures today even as I need offstage relationships in my work at Fuller Seminary.

In Numbers 20, the people of God experience another moment when the water runs out. They complain bitterly against Moses and Aaron, and Moses and Aaron go to God, who instructs them to speak to a rock and water will flow out once again. Since this is the third time in their history that God has miraculously given them water, Moses seems to be exasperated when he gathers people together to fulfill the command of God and give them water once again. But in his anger (he calls them "rebels") Moses doesn't speak to the rock but *strikes* it—*twice*. Because of this act, Moses is denied the right to enter the Promised Land. It's an odd story, and commentators disagree on why Moses was punished so harshly for *striking* rather than *speaking* to the rock to bring out the water the Israelites needed. Rabbi Jonathan Sacks believes that Moses' frustration with his people—which led him to rely on an old behavior (striking the rock) rather than a new behavior (speaking to the rock)—revealed that while he was the leader for the Israelites in the past, he would not be a good leader for their children in the future.[22]

Sacks goes on to highlight a detail in the chapter that is often overlooked. Verse 1 reads, "the whole congregation came into the Wilderness. . . . *Miriam died there, and was buried there.*" Moses defaults back to the actions of the past because his frustration was exacerbated by Miriam's death. "This was the first trial he had to face as leader of the people without the presence of his sister. . . . For the first time Moses faces a challenge without her, and for the first time Moses loses emotional control in the presence of the people."[23]

Studies of resilient leaders point to these same characteristics in offstage relationships. "The quality of your relationships with other people influences how emotionally resilient you can be in the face of an emotional or physical crisis. In general, the more quality social support you can draw upon from family and friends, the more flexible and resilient you can be in stressful situations."[24]

While it's clear that Miriam was at times a front-stage and backstage ally of Moses, her silent presence throughout his life as his older sister reminds us that all leaders need people who are more concerned about us than even the cause or the movement. For Heifetz, these are the confidants who make up a leaders' "sanctuary." They are the people who help leaders—especially when things are tough—"get back in touch with the worth of their life and the worth of their work."[25]

For Heifetz and his colleagues this is the critical difference between allies and confidants. While many of our relationships overlap, allies are *primarily* front-stage relationships and confidants are *primarily* offstage. They are usually outside of the organization; they are focused more on paying attention to, being loyal only to, and giving encouragement to the leader than they care about the organization or even a great mission. They want to build us up and can be protective of us first and foremost.[26]

While coaches and mentors function as part of the backstage, spiritual directors, psychological therapists, and support groups are invaluable to the leader as the kind of offstage sanctuary that Heifetz commends. This is also the stage where most of us experience the grace of a loving spouse and family, where our friends show up firmly on our side and encourage us to be our very best selves.

When I moved to the seminary to be part of a leadership team that was focused on bringing a significant adaptive change to theological education, I was blessed to be reunited in much closer proximity to some of our closest friends and one of my wife's dearest cousins. These are all friends who have known us our entire marriage. All were friends who were invited to a small dinner party where Beth and I celebrated our thirtieth anniversary; they all traveled across the country for our daughter's wedding. It's impossible to overstate how important it is for leaders to have these kinds of deep friendships offstage in order to perform well front stage.

One of the beautiful and complex things about leadership in a church or Christian context is how often these relationships overlap. Sometimes it can be very painful. Those who were once friends become casualties in leadership decisions. But other times it can be one of the greatest gifts for a leader.

AN ANVIL TO LAST GENERATIONS

"Reverend Bolsinger? My name is Al Sloan and I'm calling from the Pastor Nominating Committee of San Clemente Presbyterian Church."

That call in October 1996 changed my life. Not only did I end up serving as the pastor at San Clemente Presbyterian for seventeen years, but Al and his wife, Enid, became dear friends and mentors to Beth and me, and surrogate grandparents to our children.

Raised on farms in Iowa at the end of the Great Depression, Al and Enid were hardworking, loving, and caring souls. They had met in the seventh grade and were married over sixty years. After moving to California with their young family, they had both been successful real estate brokers, and Al went on to become president of the company. While they raised their son and daughter, they were volunteer youth leaders at their church and grew a youth group to over one hundred kids. They moved to our little beach town of San Clemente in retirement.

When I first arrived at the church as the new pastor, without even knowing me well, Al took me to lunch and said, "Enid and

I decided that if I was on the nominating committee then we were committing to not only help the church find the new pastor but also help the new pastor thrive here. We are committed to doing everything in our power to help you have a great ministry and a great life."

A great ministry and a great life.

Look at those words again. If you are a pastor or a leader, you probably have a lump in your throat. You know what a huge gift Al and Enid Sloan gave to Beth; our son, Brooks; our daughter, Ali; and me. Those words could have been etched on my own personal leadership anvil. Because they were the most solid elements of the truly wonderful ministry and life that we had in the seventeen years in San Clemente, raising our kids and pastoring that congregation we loved.

The very first day we arrived in San Clemente on an overcast day, in a house still filled with boxes, Al arrived to take me to the presbytery meeting where I would officially be enrolled in the presbytery. Sixty-eight-year-old Al introduced thirty-three-year-old me to every pastor and leader in the presbytery with the booming words "Come meet Tod; he's my pastor!" Meanwhile back in our rented house, Enid held our three-month-old daughter all day so Beth could unpack some boxes and start to make the semblance of a home.

Al served on the Session, became a full-time volunteer director of lay ministry at the church, wrote thousands of brightly colored postcards of encouragement (which he called "Barnabas Cards" after the early apostle first mentioned in Acts 4), and was a mentor to me as I learned to manage and lead a team. Enid was a deacon, a spiritual friend to many, and a partner to Al in reviving a senior ministry at the church. One evening a week they watched our young kids so Beth and I could have a date night. They regularly came to our home, filling it with love and laughter. Today, Al and Enid have passed away, but their legacy in my life and in the life of the two churches they served as lay leaders for most of their adult lives continues.

When we look at the lives of Al and Enid Sloan through the lens of Matt Bloom's research on flourishing in ministry, we can see just how profound their tangible support was for my leadership resilience. They were part of our onstage cast that shared the ministry leadership with me. In the years after I left San Clemente Presbyterian Church to go to Fuller Seminary to teach and train Christian leaders, they became wise backstage mentors, prayer partners, and sources of wisdom, encouragement, and, many times, challenge. Today, I have three of Al's bright Barnabas Cards in my office, the strong handwriting emphasized with underlining. "What are *you* doing for the Kingdom of God *today*, Tod?"

And keeping their pledge to help us have a great ministry and a great *life*, they were also dear offstage friends, babysitters, models for marriage, and surrogate parents and grandparents for our whole family. The last time that Beth and I were with Al, just days before he died, he took our hands, I kissed his cheek, and he mistakenly called me by his son's name. With all the intensity and energy he could summon he said, "You are *mine*. You two are *my* kids. You are *mine*." Those were the last words I ever heard from the man who made up the solid iron core of an anvil that even today holds me and grounds me in love.

IF I WERE A BISHOP . . .

I once heard someone say that "hardship + relationship = resilience." While it is clear that the development of a tempered leader is indeed a bit more complex, this is a good, simple starting point for leaders who find themselves feeling the heat of leading and the intense 2,000-degree heat of vulnerability and self-awareness that comes from reflection.

Indeed, this is so critical to both developing the tempered resilience to lead change (and even just surviving the change process) that when I am asked what advice I would give to a change leader who is beginning to feel the heat of a change, I now have a standard response.

"If I were a bishop," I say half in jest while my bishop colleagues look on in bemusement, "and I could make a pronouncement that everyone would have to follow, I would want to issue a decree that to lead alone is reckless and arrogant; it is foolish and dangerous to both self and others. To lead alone usually results in either a failure of nerve or a failure of heart, which is to squander the valuable time, energy, and commitment of organizations and followers. And therefore, to lead a people without partners and mentors, full support of family and friends, and a lifetime commitment *at every moment that you are leading* of being in either psychological therapy, coaching, spiritual direction, or mentoring would be considered *leadership malpractice.*"

This is why every doctoral student in my leading change cohort is required to do at least six months of therapy, spiritual direction, or engagement with an executive coach. This is why in my own life I have had years of executive coaching, spiritual direction, therapy, and more mentors than I can count.

When I talk to students who ask me how to find a mentor, I say, "Don't worry about finding a mentor. *Be a mentee.* Take responsibility for your life and your leadership, your growth and your formation. Let the work of leadership and the heat of self-reflection make you more self-aware and vulnerable to the place where you are feeling malleable and oozy, and humbly ask a wise person one question: 'Can I buy you a cup of coffee?' When they agree, as they usually will, then lay on the anvil and let them hold you with their advice and shape you with their questions."

Be a mentee. Show up oozy in your relationships and let them hold you when the hammering begins.

6

HAMMERING

STRESS MAKES A LEADER

The testing of your faith produces endurance; and
let endurance have its full effect, so that you may
be mature and complete, lacking in nothing.

JAMES 1:3-4

While others besides him use hammers, it is to the smith
that they all must go for their hammers. The smith, among all
mechanics, enjoys the distinction of producing his own tools.

PRACTICAL BLACKSMITHING

"THAT HAMMER IS HEAVY," the instructor said.

For Beth and me standing in front of the anvil with a pair of tongs and molten steel, the weight of the hammer and what we were going to be doing for the next couple of hours felt significant. We were enthusiastic and ready to jump in, swinging away. But our instructor warned us that a lot of wasted effort goes into something when we try to force something. In reality, the process and tools do much of the work. Besides, he said, we could pull a muscle or tire out our arms by thinking we had to add a lot of muscle to this process of heating, holding, and hammering.

The malleable, heated steel on the anvil was now ready for the hammer. One swing at a time slowly, repeatedly, over time, in a process that requires constant reheating and replacing, the steel is shaped into a tool for the task.

"Just remember," the instructor said, "you are going to be swinging that hammer over and over again. You don't have to swing it hard, just let it fall and let the hammer do the work."

Let the hammer do the work.

BECOMING A TEMPERED LEADER

Working: Leaders are formed in leading.

Heating: Strength is forged in self-reflection.

Holding: Vulnerable leadership requires relational security.

Hammering: Stress makes a leader.

Hewing: Resilience takes practice.

Tempering: Resilience comes through a rhythm of leading and not leading.

Blacksmiths may be the only ancient artisans who used their crafts to make their tools and then used their tools to ply their craft. The very act of making tools is what helped them hone their craft and turned them into the smith to whom others would come to have their tools made. Leaders may be those same artisans today. One of my friends who is both the pastor of a church and a marriage and family therapist likes to say that in anything relating to the care or leadership of humans, "You are your only tool."

As we consider what it takes for a leader to develop the tempered resilience that will withstand both a failure of nerve and a failure of heart, we will see how *stress makes a leader* when that stress *is focused on a particular formational purpose.* In other words, what gets hammered into a leader becomes the very attributes they will use to hew hope from despair.

If the goal remains to become a tempered tool that can hew stones of hope out of a mountain of despair, and if we have the right shop, a hot fire, and a safe anvil, what are the hammers that will form the tool?

To answer that question fully, we have to leave the heat of the Los Angeles blacksmithing shop and travel to the cool mountain rivers of Idaho.

> **Stress makes a leader *when that stress is* focused on a particular formational purpose.**

FISHING WITH ZACH

It was the best worst day of fly-fishing in my life. If I scroll through the pictures, there was nothing not to like. Several shots of glistening rainbows, hulking browns, and charismatic cutthroats. Smiling faces in a stunning backdrop. Beth and I spent the day catching big fish on a beautiful river that cuts majestically through a mountain canyon. What could be better?

I have been fly-fishing for almost twenty years, but like any recreational fisherperson who gets in, at most, a couple of weeks a year, I am not an expert by a long shot. So, I decided to ask a real expert for some pointers. That changed my day.

Our guide, Zach, is not just a guy who knows the local waters and can show you a few pointers. He's the head guide for all of North America for his outfitter. He's been fishing almost *every day* for *more* than twenty years. And with every one of my imprecise casts, every unproductive mend, every late hook set, every tangle, and every missed fish, he calmly, clearly, precisely corrected me, demonstrating the analytical skill of the engineering student he once was.

In one day he broke down and remade my entire approach to fly-fishing. It was exactly what I needed after years of cultivating some bad habits reinforced through the adrenaline-filled high of catching and landing fish. It was frustrating—a humbling day.

On a day that I would usually just keep celebrating the high fish count and brag-worthy pictures, I was way more aware of how much I still had to learn, how often—as experienced as I was—I did it *wrong*. So, at the end of the day, I was tired and melancholy. When my wife and our friends enthusiastically cheered each other on about one great catch after another, I sat there spent and reflective with a half-smile.

The next day I was back on the smaller river I consider my "home waters" with another friend and another guide. But today, instead of asking for more pointers, I just asked the guide to point me to some good spots on the river while he worked with my friend. I had enough lessons to practice still left over from Zach.

Deliberately, methodically, intentionally, I tried to put into practice what I had learned with Zach. I could still hear his low, calm voice in my ear. And then it all came together. A smooth, precise cast into the right spot; a gentle, quick mend of the line; and—boom!—a hard strike. Within two seconds, I was playing a big fish. The guide came over to lend his net to the cause, and after a good fight the most beautiful rainbow settled softly into the net. The guide let out a hoot. "I've been fishing this river for ten years; that's the biggest fish I have ever seen here." (I whispered a thank you to Zach under my breath.)

What I learned on that frustrating day and through Zach's clear, firm tutelage is an example of what has been termed *deliberate practice*. When the oft-quoted "10,000 hours" is cited as the path to mastery, what most forget is that it is ten thousand hours of *deliberate practice*.[1] It is ten thousand hours of *hard* work under the tutelage of an expert, focusing on the mistakes that need to be overcome, the undoing of bad habits, and the development of new skills. The key is that we sometimes have to sacrifice some of the enjoyment of the task to get better at the task. It isn't pleasant to sacrifice some of the joy of a good day fishing to get better at fishing. And the voice of the instructor, the strain to master a new task, the awkwardness of repetitively doing something that we are not already good at is hard, it is *stressful*.

It hammers away at us.

What is also often overlooked is that practice is something that we *do*, not something that we *think* about or even *pray* about. Deliberate practice is a kind of stress that we take on in our body so we can develop the poise to bring the strength and capacity formed by that stress to bear in a particular circumstance. As one of my mentors taught me, "At the moment of crisis you do not rise to the occasion, you default to your training."[2]

All practices are *embodied*; that is, they are more than a mental activity or attitude, but over time for a Christian they increase the capacity of a Christian to act more like Christ. While learning requires reflection, practice must be enacted in order to be learned. Even *spiritual* disciplines, as Dallas Willard points out, are dependent on what we do with our *bodies*.[3]

Both what I am calling spiritual practices (which shape our capacities to be a resilient Christian leader) and leadership skills (which leaders take on for the goal of forming and leading their communities to be more resilient toward change) are similar in this way. While we remain committed to reflection and relationship, if we want to grow as resilient leaders we need to retrain our brains (which are part of our bodies!)

through what we do with our hands, ears, eyes, and mouths. In the words of Dallas Willard, "A discipline is any activity within our power that we engage in to enable us to do what we cannot do by direct effort."[4]

To return to our blacksmith analogy, the hammers for shaping the raw material of a leader have *practical* but *indirect* purposes: Stress adds strength. Hammering shapes the steel into the chisel that can face the stone. In the same way, spiritual practices for a leader are not about being better at the practice itself but *forging the strength and character that has the resilience* to resist a failure of nerve and overcome a failure of heart and hew stones of hope out of a mountain of despair.

> *Spiritual practices for a leader are not about being better at the practice itself but* forging the strength and character that has the resilience *to resist a failure of nerve and overcome a failure of heart and hew stones of hope out of a mountain of despair.*

Practices, then, are not about learning intellectual concepts but developing bodily capacity. *Practices create a kind of spiritual muscle memory, training us to respond to a crisis and resistance like it is second nature.* There is a huge difference between reading a book on the value of listening to a person and letting a conversation change your mind or give you empathy. There is a chasm of difference between hearing a sermon on forgiveness and being one of the parents forgiving the man who killed five schoolgirls in an Amish community or the members the Emmanuel AME Church who *forgave* a white supremacist who shot their pastor and a group of congregants while in prayer for no other reason than because they were black.[5] Yes, we are shaped by our life experiences, our relationships, our beliefs, but so much of what creates the capacity to do repetitively the hard acts of leadership is shaped by previous actions that we have practiced numerous times.

In our vocation formation work at Fuller Seminary, Mark Lau Branson helps students see the connection between individual spiritual *disciplines* (e.g., fasting, prayer, Bible reading, and tithing) and *practices* as "clusters" of activities (like worship, community, hospitality, and formation that are made up of individual disciplines) that endure over *time* to *form characteristics* in the life of a Christian (like humility, generosity, kindness, and godliness).[6] Similarly, there are clusters of activities that we call *practices* for shaping the characteristics of a tempered, resilient leader (grounded, teachable, attuned, adaptable, tenacious) and the *deliberate* commitment to those practices that take the shape of a rule of life for change leaders.

A RULE OF LIFE FOR CHANGE LEADERS

Even before St. Benedict wrote a "rule" to give a shared structure and way of living to his companions the sixth century, Christians who have desired to be more intentional in a shared life of discipleship, mission, and spiritual formation have constructed agreements of commitments and practices. By the Middle Ages, these agreements became the rule that made up a monastic order, and today similar rules of life are used by Christians who, either individually or communally, make commitments of behaviors and practices that will serve their growth in discipleship.

In his book *Crafting a Rule of Life: An Invitation to the Well-Ordered Way*, Stephen Macchia describes a rule of life as "a

holistic description of the Spirit-empowered rhythms and relationships . . . a set of guidelines that support or enable us to
do the things we want and need to do. . . . It allows us to live
with intention and purpose in the present moment."[7] For
Benedict and other leaders of discipleship communities, the
"intention and purpose of the present moment" is usually cen-
tered on a disciplined and focused approach to spiritual growth
in Christ. Rules of life are made up of intentional spiritual practices and commitments for the purpose of serving as a trellis
that supports the branches that are connected to the vine, Jesus
(John 15), in order to have a fruitful life of discipleship. This is a
worthy pursuit that saints throughout the ages have undertaken either in community or individually to grow in Christ.

A rule of life, then, is not a set of regulations that followers
of Jesus must adhere to in order to be saved or experience
grace, but a support system that enables the disciple to respond faithfully to the grace of the Spirit in ways that further
growth and effectiveness in a life of following Jesus.

For different communities and their specific missions, the
rules will be different. And the vows and their attendant practices will therefore be different. For example, Benedictines have
a vow of stability that calls them to stay within their particular
community for life, but Jesuits have a commitment to *mobility*
that would enable them to respond to the call of God and go—
even on very short notice—wherever they needed to go for the
"greater glory of God."[8]

For Martin Luther King Jr. the demands of a nonviolent public
protest movement for racial equality and reconciliation led to
the development of a commitment or rule of life that was very
specific for furthering those ends. Every volunteer was required
to sign a commitment card that read:

I HEREBY PLEDGE MYSELF—MY PERSON AND BODY—TO THE
NONVIOLENT MOVEMENT. THEREFORE I WILL KEEP THE
FOLLOWING TEN COMMANDMENTS:

1. MEDITATE daily on the teachings and life of Jesus.
2. REMEMBER always that the nonviolent movement in Birmingham seeks justice and reconciliation—not victory.
3. WALK and TALK in the manner of love, for God is love.
4. PRAY daily to be used by God in order that all men might be free.
5. SACRIFICE personal wishes in order that all men might be free.
6. OBSERVE with both friend and foe the ordinary rules of courtesy.
7. SEEK to perform regular service for others and for the world.
8. REFRAIN from the violence of fist, tongue, or heart.
9. STRIVE to be in good spiritual and bodily health.
10. FOLLOW the directions of the movement and of the captain on a demonstration.

I sign this pledge, having seriously considered what I do and with the determination and will to persevere.[9]

A rule, therefore, is adapted to the *mission* of the group or the individual disciple. While many different practices (and disciplines) show up in spiritual formation literature, there is an overlap with leadership-development activities and exercises that, even without the religious or theological commitment, are helpful for a leader. In our case the capacity to lead change in the face of resistance requires a set of practices that a leader would take on. In other words, most rules are for a *way of living* as a Christian, but I am suggesting a rule for a *way of leading* and even more specifically for answering the question, *What practices of a rule of life form leadership resilience for facing resistance?*

The great temptation of a leader bringing an adaptive change is to default to old behaviors or quick fixes to calm the anxiety of the group. Instead of bringing genuine transformation, the leader suffers a failure of nerve and either goes back to the status quo or looks for a quick fix that exacerbates the problem. The resilience to stay in the adaptive process with one's people when they begin to become restless to either return to Egypt or to make a golden calf requires a kind of strength of will that is not mustered at the moment but must be hammered into the character of a leader.

> What practices of a rule of life form leadership resilience for facing resistance?

In the same way that a chisel is not a sledgehammer and that hewing stones is not the same thing as smashing rocks to bits, the resilient leader has a kind of focused, sharpened strength of character that shows up as being grounded, teachable, attuned, adaptable, and tenacious. Like the smith's hammering that shapes the steel, the deliberate practices are the heavy hammer that shapes the spirit and capacity of a leader to put those qualities into action when the time counts. But the thing that must be overcome in all of this is the temptation to *either give in, give up, or give a quick fix* that will appease the crowd without truly addressing the problem. The spiritual practices that make up the change leader's rule of life are specifically for hammering into the leader the very character qualities that form this capacity.

So, what are those practices? Let me suggest four that hammer in characteristics that will enable a change leader to withstand a failure of nerve and a failure of heart (see fig. 6.1).

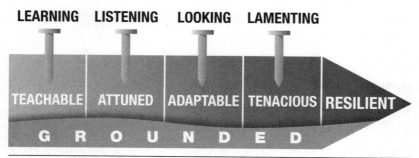

Figure 6.1. Practices that "hammer in" characteristics

LEARNING: HAMMERING IN HUMILITY

The tired clergy couple walked into a crowded banquet hall for a breakfast meeting. Over a hundred people had gathered at Fuller Seminary for our annual New Year's gathering, and there was a buzz about the speakers. They had flown throughout the night to be with us because the evening before they had led a public worship event in their home city of Bogota, Colombia, to nearly one million people. Pastors Ricardo and Ma. Patricia Rodríguez of Centro Mundial de Avivamiento, a church of one hundred thousand members that hosts a clergy leadership conference with twenty-five thousand pastors each year, traveled to this breakfast to share a testimony of what God's Spirit was doing in their country. Three times during the message they implored the gathered leaders and donors of Fuller Seminary, "We are having a revival . . . and *we need you to train us.*"

Sitting in that meeting that morning on the last day of 2017, I said to myself, *They are having a revival,* we *need them to train us.* But that was not why they had come. They had come to Fuller—amid staggering success—to ask for *help.* So many of the people being saved needed in-depth discipleship. So many of the churches being planted in a rapid movement of God throughout South America were being led by pastors with little training. As graduates of Fuller, the Rodríguezes were committed to the learning needed for their mission to continue to flourish. As leaders of a movement that was growing bigger than most of us could even imagine, they had found the grace to remain teachable, and by traveling across two continents, they demonstrated their humility. And the gathering was *stunned by it*. By all the usual markers of ministry they were having tremendous fruitfulness. Literally, hundreds of thousands of people listen to their voices and accept their wisdom and insight. Yet, at a moment of great blessing, they flew all night to ask for help so their movement could be all that God wanted it to be.

A teachable learning mindset leads to a greater capacity for standing in a difficult position, ... because there is an inherent assurance that if all else fails this trial will—if nothing else—lead to further growth. And growth as a person or a leader is of such value that it is worth the price even of failure.

Great leaders are committed learners.[10] Resilient leaders remain the most teachable. Bill Gates famously reads one book a week and Warren Buffet estimates that he spends 80 percent of his time reading. The most successful entrepreneurs of our day readily acknowledge having a coach to help them lead well.[11] And the advocates for the development of talent through "deliberate practice" insist that to achieve the level of effectiveness needed to truly be great in any field requires coaching, feedback, and ongoing instruction—even for those who are the most successful.[12]

Studies show that a critical attribute for leaders to continue to lead effectively is a teachable *learning mindset*. A learning mindset is both the belief that one *can* continue to grow and the *preference* to increase one's growth even more than enhance one's reputation or self-perception of expertise.[13] A teachable learning mindset leads to a greater capacity for staying in a difficult position, taking on a particularly difficult task or standing up to resistance, because *there is an inherent assurance that if all else fails this trial will—if nothing else—lead to further growth.* And growth as a person or a leader is of such value that it is worth the price even of failure. Or as Paul wrote to the Romans "suffering produces endurance, and endurance produces character, and character produces *hope*" (Romans 5:3-4, emphasis mine).

Lynn Ziegenfuss believes that this learning mindset is the foundational internal commitment for effective leaders. They must "own their learning and own their own needs," she said, including "taking personal responsibility for getting those learning needs met." This is why Ziegenfuss and Walter Wright define mentoring as "a voluntary relationship of self-directed *learning*." Ziegenfuss adds, "As a leader, you have to reconcile that *you* have to take responsibility for your own self-care and growth."[14] This means not only believing that we *can* grow but also acknowledging our *specific* needs for further development, having the humility to ask for help, and taking the initiative to get the instruction, coaching, or mentoring needed. In their consultation work with executives and organizations, Ziegenfuss and Wright take this concept even further, counseling organizational executives, "Don't create a mentoring program, instead create an environment of learning and ask people, 'Who would you want to help you in your learning?'"[15]

For many leaders, especially those in religious settings, this is a difficult question to ask and a learning mindset is difficult to maintain because the "expert expectation" that is projected onto religious leaders is very hard to overcome.[16] Pastors often have master's degrees or doctorates. They are expected to be the expert in biblical interpretation, church history, theology, ethics, and pastoral care. They are assumed to speak with the wisdom of God and, in every case, have clarity about the direction God is leading.

I can remember when we were facing a big decision at San Clemente Presbyterian Church, an elder in my church who was the same age as my parents said to me, "Tod, I trust that you are our pastor and that God will talk to you and through you. Whatever you decide, I believe we should do." She meant that as a statement of support, and I thanked her for it. But even then, I knew that her expectation of my wisdom ability to discern the leading of God without a pillar of cloud by day and fire by night was suspect. But actually *saying* that to her was another matter. I remember thanking her and standing there silently letting her assume that I knew perfectly what to do.

Having a learning mindset and being teachable requires that leaders acknowledge their ignorance or confusion and be open to the humble hammering of learning—especially the ability to learn from mistakes. And at that moment, the decision to be open, to become self-aware of one's defensiveness, to stop talking and focus on the learning that comes from the mistake is where a mindset turns into a practice. And the heaviest hammer—the most formative—practice is to use the heat of vulnerability and the safety of relationships, to *learn more about ourselves* from our mistakes. Jonathan Sacks writes,

I learned over the years that we make mistakes, but it is from our mistakes that we learn. You cannot get it right without first getting it wrong. If you lack the courage to fail, you will lack the courage to succeed. It is from our worst mistakes that we grow. We learn humility. We discover that you cannot please everyone. We encounter resistances, and as with the body so with the soul: it is resistance training that gives us strength. What matters is not that we succeed, but that we enter the arena, are forced to fight with the weaknesses of our nature, that we put ourselves on the line, commit ourselves to high ideals, and refuse the easy options of cynicism, disillusion, or blaming others.[17]

Again, practices are embodied. Learning mindsets need to become learning practices. And if practices are, in Mark Lau Branson's terms, "clusters of activity" that "over time" form characteristics, then what are the activities that make up the practice of learning that will form humble teachability and increase resilience? Sometimes called "spiritual disciplines," I contend that almost any embodied experience of regular learning will not only assist the leader in increasing knowledge and understanding but will also reinforce and deepen the teachable humility that is the key characteristic.

I have found that as I gain experience and am put in positions of leadership or influence, it almost doesn't matter *what* I am learning, what is critical is that I am in an actual position where I am the learner, not the expert; that I feel again the experience of being uncertain, unsure of what is needed next and in need of instruction; that I am focused on my own growth, not helping someone else grow; and that I am having to face and acknowledge my ignorance, inexperience, and need for help. Which can be done in a classroom, a conference boardroom, or right in the middle of every leadership challenge.

SOME DISCIPLINES FOR THE PRACTICE OF LEARNING

Read, listen to podcasts, and take courses—make a regular commitment.

Learn a new language.

Join a conversation where people of widely divergent backgrounds and beliefs have a meal together and discuss issues for finding connection and common ground. Make your focus to truly understand a perspective that is different than the one you have.

Travel to different cultures where you are not in the dominant majority.

Take online courses in subjects that you neglected in your formal education.

Learn a new hobby that requires you to master new abilities.

Practice reverse mentoring in which a person who is younger or less experienced is the mentor, coach, or teacher in a subject or skill that you didn't learn earlier in life. (I often joke that I could use an eleven-year-old coach to help me with all of my technology!)

CONSIDER

When was the last time you updated your spiritual practices to better form you for your leadership challenges?

LISTENING: HAMMERING IN ATTUNEMENT

We had just finished hiking twenty miles. The morning had started at Glacier Point in Yosemite National Park, had led us up through miles of forested trails, up numerous switchbacks, over hundreds of granite steps, and ascending three hundred feet of a granite incline, pulling ourselves up the backside of Half Dome using the famous installed steel cables. For twelve years, every year I took an incoming high school senior class and a group of leaders on this epic hike. Earlier in the day we had celebrated our accomplishment with lunch, cellphone calls to parents, and a group picture standing on top of Half Dome taking in the vast valley below.

And then we had nine miles to go back to the Yosemite Valley floor. Because one of the girls on the trip strained her knee, I ended up having to drop back from the rest of the group and go superslow. What should have been a three-hour trip down turned into five as we limped into Curry Village late, out of water, and very tired.

But just as I sat down to eat a piece of pizza, someone said, "Isn't Stan with you?" I was bewildered. Stan was an experienced hiker and had been at the front of the group, he should have come in long before. It didn't make sense.

"Why would Stan be with me?" I asked.

"He finished the hike with us, but he knew you were bringing the girl down, that it was getting cold and dark, and that you were running out of water. He filled up water bottles and grabbed an extra jacket and headed back up to help you. You didn't see him on the trail?"

I shook my head and felt a shiver of dread. We were all tired. It was late into the evening and dark. It was pretty dangerous for Stan to be on that trail in these conditions right now. If we had missed each other on the trail, then anything could have gone wrong. One slippery rock could mean a deadly tumble into the cold river or over the falls that roared above us.

Just then, his wife and daughters walked up, "Where's Dad?" I explained that we must have missed each other and that he was likely back on the trail. I tried to be reassuring.

"What do you think we should do?" his wife asked me. I could hear in her calm voice the simplest catch in her throat. She looked at me intensely, trying to keep her daughters from noticing the fear that was beginning to flood through her system.

"Don't worry. We'll go back to meet him and walk down with him," I said, as calmly as I could.

I grabbed some water bottles, found my college-age son, who was an experienced hiker and had come along as a leader on the trip, and enlisted one other leader who was a college athlete and trained in wilderness first aid, asking her to grab her bag. We told the rest of the group to head back to camp.

We scarfed down some food, zipped up our jackets, and started to run back up the trail. My muscles were searing from a long day. I worried a bit that these two fit collegians may have *two* middle-aged guys to carry down the mountain. For the next two hours we would march another five miles round trip back up the trail that goes toward Nevada Falls until we got the word that Stan had made it back. Relieved, we all headed back to camp with just some stories to tell.

Looking back on that night now, I think about the other options that I had besides jumping up myself and adding another five miles of hiking to the end of a fourteen-hour, twenty-mile day. Many of those alternatives may have been smarter or even safer. And make no mistake, we were exhausted. But we pressed on and found strength and stamina to go out again into the night to look for our friend. For me, the motivation came from one simple place: *I heard the catch in his wife's throat.* It was the subtlest tick, but in her calm, steady voice I could hear her fears. While my care and concern for my friend would have led me to report his absence and assist the professionals who would eventually show up to help, the catch in her throat and the fear I could see her holding back made me get up, push through exhaustion and pain to immediately do whatever I could—including enlisting my son in the search.

In the Christmas carol "O Little Town of Bethlehem," one line has always spoken to me. Reflecting on the birth of the Savior, carolist Phillips Brooks wrote, "the hopes and fears of all the years are met in Thee tonight." For the leader who needs to endure, there is very little motivation greater than actually listening to the hopes and fears of the people you are serving. Listening not only helps us to learn, but it also helps us to *feel*. Listening not only helps us to learn ideas but also to understand at a more visceral level why those ideas matter.

> *Listening not only helps us to learn ideas but also to understand at a more visceral level why those ideas matter.*

For so many leaders the primary skill set is communication. Indeed, because the capacity to speak well in front of others is both a rare skill and a fear many people have, anyone who can confidently and articulately communicate an idea, a project, a plan, or any way forward often becomes the leader. My Fuller Seminary colleague Scott Cormode always starts his classes by writing on the whiteboard "Leadership begins in listening." For Cormode, the very act of leadership demands that we always pay attention to what he calls the "longings and losses" of those "entrusted to our care."[18]

For the resilient change leader, however, we must not only listen to *our own people* but also—and especially—to the people *for whom we are changing* as a church or organization in order to address *their* longings and losses. When leaders learn to listen deeply and nondefensively to the longings and losses of the people around them—the neighbor, the one in need, the community in distress, the people being oppressed, the marginalized, the disenfranchised—then they naturally focus their efforts on the very places where they can make the greatest impact. Listening turns the attention of a leader to *other people's* pain points instead of our own institutional survival or grand projects. Listening helps us focus our energy, build momentum, and strive to make a genuine difference.

If *learning* hammers in humility that develops a grounded and teachable self, *listening*—first to God and then to others—forms the self of the leader away from self-centeredness by hammering in attunement.

For so many change leaders in so many congregations, institutions, and companies, the voices of those we are trying to serve are lost. The sounds of the internal anxiety and fears drown out the voice that invites us to make a difference. The voices of anxious faculty keep us from hearing the longings and losses of students; the voices of the church members keep us from hearing the needs of our neighbors; the voices of those within a system with power and access keep us from hearing the cries of those who are knocking on the door hoping to come in.

And the great need of the change leader is to develop the capacity to attune to both those inside and outside. Attunement to our followers means being with people in such a way that they can face the losses that change will inevitably bring to them and helping them grow as a result. Attunement is a way of accompanying people through the process of change by helping them attune to those they are changing. Attunement therefore is a dual capacity. The capacity to deeply hear the pain points of the world while also listening to the longings and losses of our people who will need to change so we can bring hope and change to the world.

Developing resilience in a leader then means being able to listen to both the needs of the world and the fears of our people and navigating those competing values to wisely discern the strategies of change and pace of change. So, how does a leader learn to attune to both the needs of the world and the fears of the followers, wisely and well? By listening even more.

By listening to *God*.

In Genesis 12, we have the story of Abram, who heard the voice of God invite him to go to a land that he would be shown and inform him that he would become the ancestor of a great family that would bless all the families of the earth. In the Christian tradition, Abram, like Mary later when the angel Gabriel appears, is described as being *chosen* by God but given a *choice* whether to heed the voice. Abram is renamed Abraham and leads his family to follow the Voice that promised to make his line a great nation and through them to bless all the families of the earth.

Listening to God, neighbors, and those entrusted to our care is more than taking in the words or even feeling the feelings but listening in such a way that leads to a new way of acting, a new way of obedience. Indeed, for the change leader facing the cacophony of voices both inviting change and resisting it, there is but one Voice that is most necessary to hear. As Henri Nouwen writes, "It is clear that we are usually surrounded by so much inner and outer noise that it is hard to truly hear our God when he is speaking to us. We have often become deaf, unable to know when God calls us and unable to understand in which direction he calls us."[19]

For Nouwen it was critical that leaders continually use spiritual disciplines to "move slowly . . . from a life filled with noisy worries to a life in which there is some free inner space . . . to listen to God and follow his guidance."[20] Change leaders listening simultaneously to the voices of their people, to those who invite us to work for change, and even more to the God who speaks in guidance and grace grow in the attunement necessary for resilient action.

SOME DISCIPLINES FOR THE PRACTICE OF LISTENING

Lectio divina. Lectio is a listening prayer that gives us space to hear the voice of God through a simple passage of Scripture, read repeatedly.[a]

The communal reading of Scripture. Listening to long passages of Scripture being read audibly in a small group. While lectio divina is focused on short passages and longer silences, communal reading of Scripture is about hearing the Word of God as a longer narrative.

Asking questions at a 2-1 ratio. I have a goal for every statement I make in a conversation or meeting to ask two questions I genuinely don't know the answer to. This is harder than it seems, but learning to ask good questions is one way to develop a greater capacity for listening and attuning to others.

Make America Dinner Again. A nationwide organization founded in the wake of the 2016 election to address the growing political and ideological divide, they host "small dinners consist[ing] of respectful conversation, guided activities, and delicious food shared among 6-10 guests who have differing political viewpoints, and our country's best interests at heart."[b] A great way to learn to listen to those that can be the hardest to hear.

[a]Fuller Seminary has developed a website to make the communal reading of Scripture accessible and easy for any group. See "Communal Reading of Scripture," *Fuller Studio,* https://fullerstudio.fuller.edu/series/communal-reading-scripture. My favorite way of practicing lectio divina is through the British Jesuits' website Pray as You Go, https://pray-as-you-go.org.

[b]"What's MADA?" *Make America Dinner Again,* accessed April 7, 2020, www.makeamerica dinneragain.com.

LOOKING: HAMMERING IN ADAPTABILITY

In the documentary film *The Biggest Little Farm in the World*, John and Molly Chester tell the story of how over a decade they transformed a barren piece of land with dirt that was nothing more than hardened clay into a verdant and fruitful wonderland of biodiversity and completely organic farm with rich, loamy soil teeming with nine billion organisms. This process was not only filled with hard work and heartache but one constant struggle with one invasive plant, bug, snail, or predator after another. As soon as they figured out how to deal with snails, they had gophers that ate the fruit tree roots. And not only gophers but maggots that caused a fly infestation, aphids that infested their plants, birds that ate their fruit, and coyotes that attacked their chickens.

After trying one particularly disturbing but completely understandable intervention to stop the coyotes, John learned that he needed *not* to react but to learn to see the bigger system at work. First observing the way his dog, Todd, seems to look at the world, John explains:

> I feel like Todd is constantly staring deeply at these almost infinitesimal details, like he's decoding how the world around him works. So, I've started doing the same. . . . So with every new problem that popped up, I'd first take a step back and watch it. . . . Observation followed by creativity is becoming our greatest ally.

"Observation followed by creativity." Since Ronald Heifetz is a trained medical doctor, it's not surprising that the primary practice for adaptive leadership is not to *do* but first to *diagnose*. Observations always precede interpretations and interventions. The key process when someone experiences a setback or problem is to first step back and look at the problem. "To diagnose a system or yourself while in the midst of action requires the ability to achieve some distance from those on-the-ground events," Heifetz and his colleagues write.[21] They refer to this pattern of stepping back as "getting up on the balcony," comparing it to "listening on the dance floor." On the balcony we gain perspective, and on the dance floor we experience the relational intensity of the moment.

> When you move back and forth between balcony and dance floor, you can continually assess what is happening in your organization and take corrective midcourse action. If you perfect this skill, you might even be able to do both simultaneously: keeping one eye on the events happening immediately around you and the other eye on the larger patterns and dynamics.[22]

Note, that John Chester and Ronald Heifetz are both interested in actions, in making decisions, in moving the system forward. Leadership requires making judgment calls that are often risky and then taking the wisest-possible actions. But since "to lead is to decide," the tempered leader focuses *first* not on action but on observation *for* the action.[23]

In *The Biggest Little Farm in the World*, one of the most poignant moments in the film is when the coyotes have—once again—found their way into the chicken coop and killed dozens of chickens. At the time, John and Molly's primary cash product was the fresh eggs they sold at farmers' markets. To keep losing so many chickens was to risk losing the whole farm. As John and an assistant survey the grim scene, the younger woman looks to her boss and says with obvious irritation, "Are we gonna just keep letting this happen?"

John sits there crestfallen and thinking. But soon he is trying *another* experiment. He'll try to train two Great Pyrenees pups to *guard* but *not chase* the chickens. And the first results are not promising. But unless he wants to kill all the coyotes and therefore violate one of his core principles, he has to keep observing, experimenting, and learning. Even if there is a high cost to it.

Because a default response for most leaders is to immediately act, the discipline of learning to look, gain greater perspective, and understand the bigger picture *in the midst of action* is a critical skill both for wise action and for developing resilience. Maintaining one's principles in the face of adversity create inner fortitude to carry on. But even more, perspective fosters a greater sense of purpose. Seeing the bigger picture and the dynamics at play enables us to make meaning and see patterns in what would otherwise be an anxious swirl of emotions and reactions. This is especially important when the necessary change work is overwhelming because the whirl of activity, energy, and even internal emotional reaction often triggers a flight or fight response that disrupts learning by distracting us with fruitless *doing*.

Again, creativity to face problems depends on observation *first*.

In his book on developing awareness of cultural identity, *White Awake*, author Daniel Hill encourages leaders who have been shaped by the privilege of being born into the dominant culture to resist the urge to immediately try to solve problems they very likely have no capacity to understand fully. Sharing his own story of being a white pastor from a megachurch who wanted to start a multiethnic congregation that would be intentionally involved in racial reconciliation work, Hill was stunned when leaders of color suggested that he had far more to learn than to offer and that his experience in a wealthy, large church had not prepared him for the well-intended calling he had assumed. Hill shares his journey in detail, and using the story of Jesus needing to touch a man *twice* to bring healing (Mark 8:22-25), he describes the partial blindness of most leaders who come from the dominant culture and privileged backgrounds. Those leaders, Hill asserts, need to focus not on the question, What am I supposed to *do*? but instead, What do I *see*?[24]

For the leader, an emphasis on "seeing not solving" is very difficult. Most leaders have a necessary bias to action that urges them onward, but the resilient leader understands that gaining perspective, seeing the bigger picture, hearing the "music beneath the words" (the unspoken fears and anxieties, power plays, and disruptive movements that are fueling the systems' current functioning) is a critical practice for leading wise change. Like Todd, the watchful farm dog, a doctor searching for a diagnosis, or a leader "on the balcony," looking is necessary for enduring.

> *An emphasis on "seeing not solving" is very difficult. Most leaders have a necessary bias to action that urges them onward, but the resilient leader understands that gaining perspective . . . is a critical practice for leading wise change.*

The key attribute for being a good, adaptive leader is the ability to resist default reactions to crises and instead to pause to make as many observations and gather as many interpretations as possible to see the issue at hand in all of its complexity.[25] Heifetz and his colleagues offer some concrete balcony steps:

Observe what is going on around you. Stay diagnostic even as you take action. Develop more than one interpretation. Watch for patterns. Reality test your interpretation when it is self-serving or close to your default. Debrief with partners as often as you can to assess the information generated by your actions, and the interventions of others, in order to think through your next move.[26]

But to be most effective this process includes both looking from the balcony *and* listening on the floor. "When you move back and forth between balcony and dance floor, you can continually assess what is happening in your organization and take corrective midcourse action."[27]

Even more, finding meaning and being able to create innovative solutions, that make even halting progress, out of the challenges of the moments, creates the momentum to keep us going. When coaching leaders, I often give them a choice: If you had to do a ten-mile hike, would you rather do it outside going up a mountain trail or inside on a treadmill set at a steep incline? Most would opt, even if it was much harder, for the mountain trail. Why? Because we can endure much more when there is both perspective (a great view) and progress (actually going somewhere). The sense that we are laboring hard to just run in place is wearisome and demoralizing.

Learning to pause and see the moment like the complex chessboard that it is contributes to the capacity to withstand the temptations to return to the status quo or succumb to reflexive reactions and stay engaged in facing resistance. Seeing the overall emotional dynamics, the political positioning of many, the new potential for creativity, and the possibilities that are only beginning to ripen into fresh possibilities for continued creative responses gives us hope.

SOME DISCIPLINES FOR THE PRACTICE OF LOOKING

A "balcony journal." Writing a kind of after-action report of a conversation, leadership event, or conflict by writing about it three times in three different ways. The first time, write a first-person account that focuses on the feelings and experiences of being in the swirl of the dance floor. Then after setting it aside for a bit, return and rewrite it from the third person as if you are watching yourself from the balcony. Then after letting it sit again, write a coaching note to yourself about the next steps for leading through that circumstance.

Whenever you have a leadership experience that creates a feeling of being overwhelmed by the energy on the dance floor, ask a trusted coach or mentor to have a balcony conversation to help you gain perspective and to see some of the larger systems or patterns of behavior that trigger your feelings.

LAMENTING: HAMMERING IN TENACITY

Adaptive change by definition requires learning and results in loss. While we have discussed the necessity of cultivating a learning mindset, being teachable, and taking on the humility that comes from practices of learning, in real experience it is the reality of loss and the desire to avoid that loss that triggers the most significant resistance. This is true as much for leaders as for the people they lead. Leading change is leading people through loss, and it usually results in as much loss—loss of respect, loss of affection, loss of trust, even loss of position or job—sometimes, yes, loss of life—for the leader as it does for the people being led.

So how does a leader develop the tenacity to endure through loss? By intentionally leaning into loss, embracing loss, and even understanding that it is in facing the necessary losses for the desired change that the transformation process begins. As Jesus said to his disciples, "Very truly, I tell you, unless a grain of wheat falls into the earth and dies, it remains just a single grain; but if it dies, it bears much fruit" (John 12:24).

For Jim Collins, leading change does not begin in a vision but in a disciplined process of "confronting the brutal facts."[28] For Collins, much like the Silicon Valley leaders who challenged my inward, institutionally focused approach to innovation, the genesis of change is not our inspired ideas but the pain, problems, brokenness, and challenges we see in the world and our organization. Change leaders don't arise from a great vision, they are raised to meet a great need. And when leaders gather people to address the brutal facts, the first response is not to react but to become reflective so that our actions come from a deeper attunement to the greater context and condition of the pain.

For Dr. King, the inspiration for the 1963 march and the theme of the speech was not in the first sense about a dream but instead about a broken promise. He and the other civil rights leaders who gathered on the mall in front of the Lincoln Memorial in Washington, DC, had come to an event called "the March on Washington for Jobs and Freedom." Dr. King's speech was to make clear the way that African American citizens of the United States had been given promises that even one hundred years after the abolition of slavery had not been kept. For Dr. King, it was like an entire race of American citizens had been given a check by the United States that had been returned "insufficient funds." So, they had come, they said, to "make real the promises of democracy" by calling out the injustice and the despair that came from a century of broken and unfulfilled promissory notes.

> One hundred years later, the Negro is still languished in the corners of American society and finds himself in exile in his own land. And so we've come here today to dramatize a shameful condition.

In a sense we've come to our nation's capital to cash a check. When the architects of our republic wrote the magnificent words of the Constitution and the Declaration of Independence, they were signing a promissory note to which every American was to fall heir. This note was a promise that all men, yes, black men as well as white men, would be guaranteed the unalienable rights of life, liberty, and the pursuit of happiness. It is obvious today that America has defaulted on this promissory note insofar as her citizens of color are concerned. Instead of honoring this sacred obligation, America has given the Negro people a bad check, a check which has come back marked insufficient funds.[29]

Resilient change leaders cannot be Pollyannas. As James Stockdale learned as a prisoner of war in Vietnam, the optimists break first. Resilience requires a capacity to look the brutal facts square in the eye, to name the mountain of despair, and to keep hammering away with your tempered chisel.

For change leaders the practice for addressing the uncomfortable and brutal reality of the suffering of our neighbors and the pain of our friends without losing hope means bringing God—with the same brutal honesty—into our experiences. In biblical language this is called the spiritual practice of lament. It is the "language of suffering," theologian Soong-Chan Rah explains as he helps us understand this most honest, and often disturbing, type of prayer.[30]

> *For change leaders the practice for addressing the uncomfortable and brutal reality of the suffering of our neighbors and the pain of our friends without losing hope means bring God—with the same brutal honesty—into our experiences.*

Laments are prayers of petition arising out of need. But lament is not simply the presentation of a list of complaints, nor merely the expression of sadness over difficult circumstances. Lament in the Bible is a liturgical response to the reality of suffering and engages God in the context of pain and trouble. The hope of lament is that God would respond to human suffering that is wholeheartedly communicated through lament.[31]

Laments are prayers that face the brutal facts of our world, the pain points of our lives, and the challenges of our callings, and invites God right into the swirl of that disturbing moment as the one who is the primary and responsible actor during each crisis. Laments remind us that our capacity to lead in the world, especially when leading at the place of despair, resistance, and the failures of nerve and heart, is met with the power of the God who is present and is active. The change leader is made stronger, like Jacob, through brutally *honest* wrestling with God in prayer about the brutal facts of our lives. As Old Testament scholar John Goldingay says, "The psalms give a lot of space to describing, protesting, and lamenting . . . the psalms are very *general* in what we ask God to *do*, and very *detailed* about our *need*."[32]

While there is an entire book of the Bible (Lamentations) named for the prayers of lament, and while the book of Jeremiah is made up mostly of lament, the most accessible prayers of lament are in the Psalms. Psalm 22, 44, 60, 74, 79, 80, 85, and 90 represent a pattern of prayer that gets "proximate to suffering,"[33] "confronts the brutal facts,"[34] and then comes to God with the complaint. Psalm 22 is a good example of a prayer of lament that follows this biblical pattern:

- Personal address: "My God, My God. . . ." (v. 1)

- Complaint: "Why have you forsaken me? Why are you so far from helping me, from the words of my groaning?" (v. 1)

- Confession of trust: "Yet you are holy, enthroned in the praises of Israel. In you our ancestors trusted; they trusted, and you delivered them." (vv. 3-4)

- Petition: "Do not be far from me, for trouble is near and there is no one to help." (v. 11)

- Vow of praise: "I will tell of your name to my brothers and sisters; in the midst of the congregation I will praise you." (v. 22)

Like the Stockdale Paradox ("Retain absolute faith that you can and will prevail in the end, regardless of the difficulties, and at the same time, exercise the discipline to confront the most brutal facts of your current reality, whatever they might be"),[35] laments are powerful leadership tools because they reinforce to those leading the change that the way to avoid both failure of nerve and failure of heart is not to deny the mountain of despair but to confront it head-on with honesty and hope, with courage and urgency. The very attributes of a faithful lament. Dr. King again:

> But we refuse to believe that the bank of justice is bankrupt. We refuse to believe that there are insufficient funds in the great vaults of opportunity of this nation. And so we've come to cash this check, a check that will give us upon demand the riches of freedom and the security of justice. . . . Now is the time to make real the promises of democracy. Now is the time to rise from the dark and desolate valley of segregation to the sunlit path of racial justice. Now is the time to lift our nation from the quicksands of racial injustice to the solid rock of brotherhood. Now is the time to make justice a reality for all of God's children.[36]

In fall 2019, Christine Lee, the first ordained Korean-American woman priest in the Episcopal Church became the priest-in-charge of a once robust but now struggling parish in the Chelsea district of New York City. During a summer sabbatical to prepare for assuming the responsibility of bringing renewal to a church that was on the brink of dissolution, she found herself wrestling with a sense of dread and fear about leading the change process. She confronted the reality that she could fail and with her the congregation would die. She knew that bringing change would be difficult. She wrestled with God in prayer and felt an odd identification with Jesus' words of lament at Gethsemane when he wrestled with the death he was about to undergo.[37] She found herself comforted by the brutal words of Hebrews reminding her of the one "who for the sake of the joy that was set before him endured the cross, disregarding its shame" (Hebrews 12:2). "I finally had to rest," she said, "in the assurance that even if I wasn't sure I wanted what was before me, I believed that something good would happen *within me*."[38] Christine Lee's resolve and hope—and if nothing else, her own transformation—become a statement of trust in the face of the brutal facts of a challenging leadership calling.

Laments hammer tenacity into us through causing us to learn to trust God in the middle of the leadership crucible. They teach us to be both more honest and more open to the reality that God is at work even when we are bewildered and bedeviled by the brutality of pain and opposition. By acknowledging the brutal facts of a situation and letting them lead us into prayers of lament, we galvanize the energy that brings resilience, reinforces even the smallest movement of momentum, and staves off cynicism. Laments are acts of faith that strengthen the one praying for faithful, persistent, and tenacious action. What we have learned from the black freedom struggle, civil rights leaders, and others who have struggled in the face of deep, systemic resistance is the power of lament to sustain resilience. When Dr. King looked out on the crowd gathered on the Washington Mall, he could see their faces and name the pain of the gathered people, mindful, he said, that some "have come here out of great trial" that others had come "fresh from narrow jail cells," and that many, like those who had for decades labored for racial justice, had been "battered by the storms of persecution . . . and police brutality." Through the honest words of lament, he offered a charge to tenacious endurance.

> You have been the veterans of creative suffering. Continue to work with the faith that unearned suffering is redemptive. Go back to Mississippi, go back to Alabama, go back to South Carolina, go back to Georgia, go back to Louisiana, go back to the slums and ghettos of our northern cities, knowing that somehow this situation can and will be changed. Let us not wallow in the valley of despair.[39]

Understood in this way, Martin Luther King Jr.'s speech that August day that began with the image of a bad check and ended with a soaring dream was a classic lament. The theme was an honest reckoning of the debt that white America owed its black citizens. But it was not just a protest; it was a proclamation. And as a lament it did what laments do, it energized a movement to continue.

"With this faith, I go back to the south." King's voice sang out. And so he did.

SOME DISCIPLINES FOR THE PRACTICE OF LAMENTING

"Get proximate to people who are suffering." These words of justice advocate Bryan Stevenson in his 2018 commencement address at Bates College challenges us to fight against our tendency to distance and deny the pain of the world, by intentionally moving closer to people who are experiencing lament-worthy conditions.[a]

Regularly read the Psalms of Lament. Use the pattern of a lament to write a lament of your own, putting the pain of the people you are trying to serve and the people you are leading and their concerns into the texts. If you are a pastor, add prayers of lament regularly into your worship service.

Practice the discipline of learning to "see, not solve" a problem. Particularly when confronting the brutal facts of the pain points of the people around you—and don't do anything yet. See (not solve), lament first, and let those laments do their work in you.

[a]Doug Hubley, "'Get Proximate to People Who Are Suffering,' Bryan Stevenson Tells Bates Commencement Audience," *Bates College News*, May 27, 2018, www.bates.edu/news/2018/05/27/get-proximate-to-people-who-are-suffering-bryan-stevenson-tells-bates-college-commencement-audience.

7

HEWING

RESILIENCE TAKES PRACTICE

We ... boast in our sufferings, knowing that suffering
produces endurance, and endurance produces character, and
character produces hope, and hope does not disappoint us.

R OMANS 5:3-5

Leadership should generate capacity, not dependency.

R ONALD H EIFETZ

B Y THE END OF THE BLACKSMITHING CLASS, I had made
a perfectly good bottle opener. A little lopsided, yes, but
it's pretty impressive for a beginner. It has a few creative twists
in the shank and a tip that perfectly slips under a bottle cap so
I can use the curve (all of which *l* shaped) to lever the drink
open. I smile every time that I do. What was once just a rod of
steel was transformed through heating, holding, and hammering into a tool I can use around the house. And it's kind of
beautiful too.

That's the magic of blacksmithing. While you can certainly
work in hot metal for pieces of art to hang on a wall or put

on a shelf, you can also make a piece of art that can be put to good use. And if you are a blacksmith, the very tools that are made by the fire, anvil, and hammer become the tools that you can use to *make* more good things or *do* more good things.

In this chapter we move from the process of forging steel into a tool that has the strength to hew hope from despair to using that very tool (ourselves!) to shape the resilience and adaptive capacity of our congregations, organizations, and institutions. If "you are your only tool," then how do you put yourself to work shaping your people? If leadership is about generating capacity and not dependency, then how can we lead in such a way that grows the capacity of our people?[1]

How do we shape the very people who are often themselves part of the resistant, sabotaging core, into a people who can grow and face their biggest challenges and thrive?[2]

BECOMING A TEMPERED LEADER

Working: Leaders are formed in leading.

Heating: Strength is forged in self-reflection.

Holding: Vulnerable leadership requires relational security.

Hammering: Stress makes a leader.

Hewing: Resilience takes practice.

Tempering: Resilience comes through a rhythm of leading and not leading.

The ultimate goal of adaptive change is not to master a pain-free solution to a pressing problem, it's to create adaptive capacity: the wisdom, courage, and resilience within a people to learn and survive the losses necessary to be transformed and thrive in a changing world. Heifetz, in an introduction to Jonathan Sack's commentary on the Torah, asks,

> In biblical terms, we might ask how a culture of dependency can transform into a culture of widely distributed leadership, how a people enslaved for generations can become a society in which all members are called upon to take responsibility whenever they see fit, whoever they are.[3]

If resilient leadership is about taking responsibility to face often brutal reality with hope, to find meaning in setbacks, to use creative adaptations to work through challenges, and to overcome both a failure of nerve that will shrink back and a failure of heart that devolves into cynicism, how do resilient leaders form a resilient people? *The same principles apply.*

- A group is formed for bringing change because of *challenges* facing the organization.
- The group needs to develop and reaffirm a clear, *grounded*, organizational identity and mission, and grow in the capacity to be *teachable, attuned, adaptable, and tenacious.*
- The group needs to be able to practice vulnerable *reflection* and experience the trust and safety of strong, supportive *relationships.*
- The group needs to be led through the change by a resilient leader who regularly practices and demonstrates the value of *learning, listening, looking, and lamenting.*

But a set of leadership *skills* are also needed for leading change. These are the skills for the *practice of tempered change leadership,* and when exercised wisely and well they not only increase the odds for bringing change but form a more resilient people to face those odds, whatever they may be (see fig. 7.1). And nothing

creates more resilience *within a leader* than to be surrounded by
and work with resilient people toward missional goals that inspired the need for change in the first place.

MANAGING REACTIVITY

I knew something was wrong when the bishop's assistant ap-
proached me right before I was to step up to the microphone.
"We will be delayed a few minutes," he said. "Some of our pastors
are meeting with the bishop. You should know that they are
uncomfortable with your use of two slaveholders, Meriwether
Lewis and William Clark, as examples of leadership."

I nodded and swallowed hard.

I had been asked to travel to up-
state New York to speak to a group
of Methodist clergy on the topic of
leading in a rapidly changing
world. A number of the regional
leaders had read my book *Canoeing
the Mountains*, and they asked me
to be the keynote speaker for their
annual conference. In the previous
four years, I had traveled to speak
to the most diverse groups of
Christian leaders imaginable on

*Nothing creates
more resilience
within a leader than
to be surrounded
by and work with
resilient people
toward missional
goals that inspired
the need for change
in the first place.*

the story of how Lewis and Clark had to lead their Corps of
Discovery into the uncharted territory of the west. For some it
was just a historical metaphor for discussing how to lead
adaptive change. For many others, however, the very topic was
a painful reminder of the racism that makes up what Jim Wallis
has called "America's original sin."[4] And even though the hero
of the story is the Shoshone nursing mother Sacagawea, the

very fact that Lewis and Clark were slave masters and that their expedition paved the way for others to come and the eventual destruction of the way of life and relocation of the indigenous peoples of the American west is deeply troubling.

Preparing to step in front of the lectern, I mentally rearranged my outline so that we talked about the sensitive subject right up front. I wanted them to know I was using the historical figures not as models but as mirrors. I held them up because they were a lot like us, with our deep contradictions, and like us their intentions for leading were distorted and led to unanticipated consequences that they couldn't control.

And sure enough, as soon as I started in on the narrative of the travels of the Corps of Discovery, a pastor in the back of the room stood up to gain attention. When I asked her to please speak, she passionately shared the deep concern and even hurt of the group of African American clergy in the room. The ensuing conversation not only disrupted my presentation but the whole conference. The tension in the room was palpable, with one group after another threatening to leave. Some because they found the topic offensive, others because they found the protest indefensible. And there I stood in the room, the focus of a heated discussion that was directed at me but fueled by the clergy in the room who had long felt that their concerns as people of color had been ignored or minimized.

Through a long, emotional, and turbulent morning that spilled over into the afternoon, I was in the middle of a painful discussion on one of the most fraught and difficult topics. I did my best to empathize and hold the group together, but mostly what I had to work on was managing my reactivity. Tempers were high, accusations were flying, my work was being discredited, my very character was being questioned. I was aware of every word I was saying and trying to monitor even the tone of my voice. I remember telling myself to exhale, to relax my tense back muscles, to try to carefully listen to the pain that was filling the room. As I listened deeply to the people who were so understandably angry, I focused on keeping my defensiveness at bay, remembering that most of the anger wasn't directed at me personally but at the larger issues that were not only important but worthy of angry responses.

At the break I called Steve, my coach who was helping me develop cultural humility, to reflect on what I was trying to do. He asked me questions and reminded me of what it takes to create a "holding environment" that creates both safety and the ability to allow the heat of the moment to bring transformation.[5] Even talking to him helped me to relax, to remember not to take things personally, to stay attuned to both the voices of those who were protesting my presentation and those who wanted me to ignore them and continue.

The skills for leading change through the opposition, just like the process for forming a resilient leader, begin in the leader's self-awareness and self-management. The first step is managing one's reactivity in the face of internal and external opposition and sabotage.

When we reconvened, I felt more prepared to facilitate a conversation that this group of pastors needed to have even if my presentation had been the match that lit the fuse. At lunchtime, a group of Korean-American clergy who had been very frustrated by what they perceived was a "lack of respect" for me as a guest and teacher asked me to have a meal with them. They shared with me that observing my capacity to stay in the conversation and give room to the dissenting voices had been a learning moment for them too. I thanked them for their concern for me and told them that I believed most people would have understood if I had become defensive. I probably would have been forgiven if I had lashed out in frustration or used my position in the room to silence those who were protesting (indeed some were disappointed in me that I *didn't* shut them down). But that wouldn't have accomplished the reason why I had flown across the country to speak and equip leaders for adaptive change. Defensiveness, reacting, and power plays may make us feel good, but if we are truly trying to build the adaptive capacity in the room, then we have to manage our reactivity and, in the words of Ronald Heifetz, "give the work back to the people."[6]

Managing reactivity is one of the greatest challenges for me as a leader. I'm passionate, headstrong, and decisive. I'm an Enneagram Eight, sometimes known as a Challenger. I often joke that "I don't have to kick down every door, just the ones that are closed." In high school I was the captain of the wrestling team. I can easily relate to Jacob, who wrestled with God, and to Theodore Roosevelt's "man in the arena" who sees life as a struggle. If I am not at my best, I can too easily flash anger that makes the situation worse. But this time, by the grace of God and years of practice, I was able to manage my own reactivity, and help the group turn the attention away from my presentations and toward their very real and present issues. Which is far more important than how I was—or was not—treated.

By also managing my reactivity, I could hear, far more clearly than I had before, how my presentations and the themes of a book that had been mostly well-received in some circles also caused pain for my brothers and sisters from different backgrounds than my place of cultural privilege. It caused me to change my presentation, to more clearly acknowledge the

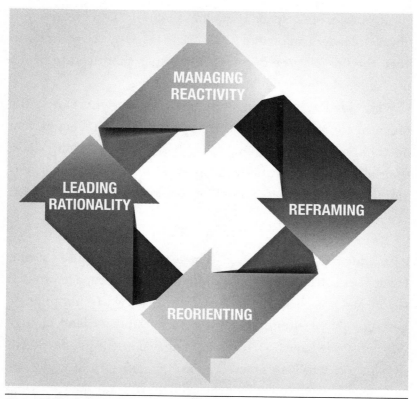

Figure 7.1. The process for "hewing" resilient organizational transformation

problematic nature of using historical figures, and state up-front that I want to continue to learn even as I help others learn.

Because so much of the process of leading change is about loss, fear, and even sabotage, it is natural, normal, and to be expected that emotions will run high. Indeed, the very crucible of the change process, the resistance of those in power, the frustration of those who are trying to bring change, and fear of those who want relational peace at any cost, means that the leader becomes the focal point for criticism from all directions. Conflict is the very process that brings change, and the only way to make the conflict healthy is for the leader to be able to create a safe, open space that allows courage and creativity to flow. For leaders, managing their own reactivity is necessary to keep the focus of the group on the issues that need to be addressed and the change process continuing.

When leaders can manage their own reactivity, slowly the focus of the conversation turns back to the challenges that need to be solved together. Slowly everyone's breathing slows, their ability to think about complex issues together sharpens, and their capacity to *see* possibilities expands.

REFRAMING

It is almost a sine qua non that leadership requires vision. Leaders are often chosen and validated by their capacity to cast vision, and it is clear that without the capacity to communicate a compelling vision, it is almost impossible to lead change. Proverbs 29:18 says, "Where there is no vision, the people perish" (KJV). And while this verse refers specifically to vision as prophecy or divine guidance, the need for the presence of strong human communication of that divine direction is still critical.

The imagery at the root of the words for "vision" and "perish" in Proverbs 29:18 is found in Exodus 32 when Moses is with God for forty days on Sinai. In his absence the people become highly anxious. Did Moses die? Who will be our leader? What should we do? In their anxiety they turn to Aaron for a solution, and he gives them a quick fix, instructing them to make for themselves a god that they can keep with them at all times. Aaron made a golden calf out of their molten jewelry and the people declared, "These are your gods, O Israel, who brought you up out of the land of Egypt!" In a moment of deep anxiety, without the voice of their prophet and the presence of their leader in their midst, the people turn on Moses and turn on God.

This harrowing passage speaks of the necessity for the people of God to have in their midst both the guidance of the word of God and the voice of the leader continually pointing them to their identity and mission. When a people lose the voice and vision of the leader—even for a short time—they are susceptible to the kind of corporate failure of nerve that turns a community into a mob that will do anything to bring them security and lower their anxiety. They look for quick-fix solutions and often do so even to the point of compromising all that makes them who they are. Soon, what was once a great community is stumbling toward ruin.

Christianity is faith and practice as a response to the saving grace of God. That grace is demonstrated in the life, death, and resurrection of Jesus Christ in the historical past, that provides the compelling narrative for living out the Christian faith and for leading communities of Christian faith. In other words, God's activity in the past is the first fruits of a future vision of a redeemed and renewed world (Acts 1:8).

Indeed, the primary prayer and vision of the Christian come from the heart of the prayer Jesus taught his first followers, who pray to the Father in heaven with the words, "Your kingdom come, your will be done, on earth as it is in heaven." In the

> *"Therefore we do not lose heart. Though outwardly we are wasting away, yet inwardly we are being renewed day by day. For our light and momentary troubles are achieving for us an eternal glory that far outweighs them all. So we fix our eyes not on what is seen, but on what is unseen, since what is seen is temporary, but what is unseen is eternal."*
> 2 Corinthians 4:16-18 NIV

words of institution for the Lord's Supper, the central sacramental practice of the church, we are reminded that what Jesus did on the cross is the motivation for his followers to remain unified in the witness and work of Jesus, in the fellowship and mission of Jesus, "until he comes again."

For Paul that vision of the eternal kingdom that is to come on earth as it is in heaven is what enables day-to-day resilience.

> So we do not lose heart. Even though our outer nature is wasting away, our inner nature is being renewed day by day. For this slight momentary affliction is preparing us for an eternal weight of glory beyond all measure, because we look not at what can be seen but at what cannot be seen; for what can be seen is temporary, but what cannot be seen is eternal. (2 Corinthians 4:16-18)

And a vision of what is not yet before us, but that we can "see" with eyes of faith, hope, and imagination—when captured and cast—creates the shared motivation for confronting resistance and continuing tenaciously toward the larger transformative goal. In the same way that Martin Luther King Jr.'s address at the Lincoln Memorial shared a vision for the hundreds of thousands gathered (and many more millions since who have seen the video) that created hope for returning to the work of bringing civil rights to all Americans, Edwin Friedman drew upon that same visionary speech when he was consulting with leaders who were bogged down and disoriented by the resistance they were facing. He wrote that there was a similarity to their stories where they became mired in moments of despair and defensiveness. They became stuck, burned out, or had begun to give in to the most dysfunctional forces in the system.

In short, they had forgotten to lead. I therefore stopped listening to the content of everyone's complaints and, irrespective of the location of their problem or the nature of their institution, began saying the exact same thing to everyone: *"You have to get up before your people and give an "'I Have a Dream' speech."*[7]

Friedman discovered that whether or not the leaders' own "I Have a Dream Speech" rallied the community to a shared vision, just articulating the vision energized *the leaders*. The act of *reframing* a people's history for the present moment and casting a vision of change created focus, clarity, and self-definition for the leaders who would often renew their calling to be, in Friedman's words, "the strength in the system."

In an adaptive change process, vision is usually not about a *new* vision but a *renewed* vision. It is helping people see what they have missed and recover their best intentions and dreams that have become set aside or discarded and then adapted to a new day. It creates the energy of an aha! moment, seeing something that had been previously unseen that gives new perspective and leads to new energy that can then be deployed through a clear call to action.[8] Since adaptive change is about responding to a changing environment with healthy adaptation of an organization or community's core values and reason for being, then communicating vision is more about recovery and *reframing* than it is about discovering something new.

When Alan Mulally became Ford Motor Company's CEO in September 2006, the company was in the middle of the worst year in their long history. They posted a $12.7 billion loss for the year, and most industry and financial leaders expected Ford to soon file for bankruptcy. The iconic company was in deep trouble borne of the complacency and mission drift that often follows a long season of being an undisputed industry leader.

Now, with competition coming from global car companies, its own cars being widely criticized for being an inferior product, and the internal company culture so siloed and toxic that one unit competed against another, Mulally faced a daunting task.

On the eve of his retirement in July 2014, having brought back Ford from the brink of corporate death in a leadership feat that has been hailed as a "history-making revitalization," Mulally was asked what made the difference. Of all the factors that Mulally is now famous for implementing, he focused on one: "What I've learned is the power of a compelling vision."[9] Indeed, for Mulally that was his first priority. "The first thing that I wanted to do was to pull everybody together around a compelling vision, and I found that in Henry Ford's original vision."[10]

Mulally's approach is a sublime example of the kind of visionary leadership that is required to bring adaptive change. Adaptive leadership is not finding a new inspiring vision but *reframing* an original or enduring vision of the organization that allows everyone to see a new, compelling future for their beloved organization that is worth sacrifice and commitment.

For Mulally, saving a complex, multinational, century-old company with both legacy stakeholders and an entrenched corporate culture started with two words: *One Ford*. "One Ford" meant recapturing Henry Ford's original vision from 1925 of "Opening the highways to all mankind" and helping everyone in the company see that by coming together around a shared vision, they contribute to a better world.[11]

For Alan Mulally "One Ford" became the central vision for doing many deeply complex and difficult tasks, including a massive realignment in their products, operations, and structures. "One Ford" led them to sell off luxury brands (that the Ford family members loved to drive and were proud to claim as their own), and "One Ford" became the rallying cry for changing a corporate culture that had become so defensive that senior company leaders regularly kept key information from each other to strengthen their own standing in the company.

Those two words were embedded in Mulally's conversations, meetings, emails, and interviews every day. He even famously carried those words with him on a laminated card. One interviewer observed, "Mulally repeated the One Ford mantra until many journalists and analysts were tired of hearing it, yet One Ford permeated the culture and triggered creative, innovative ideas."[12]

Adaptive leadership is not finding a new inspiring vision but reframing an original or enduring vision of the organization that allows everyone to see a new, compelling future for their beloved organization that is worth sacrifice and commitment.

When Fuller Seminary was trying to discern the future of theological education for a rapidly changing world, we revisited our past. Two trained consultants took us through a time line of the most significant events in our institutional history. We told story after story and kept finding a quality that we labeled the "trailblazing marriage of unlikely partners," something that started at Fuller's founding when it was originally constituted out of the shared vision of two founders, not one.

Harold John Ockenga, the first president of Fuller, was an East Coast academic and pastor of the historic Park Street Church in Boston, Massachusetts, and Charles E. Fuller was a West Coast radio evangelist who at his peak had ten million listeners every week tuning in to the "Old Fashioned Revival Hour." As we were working on the future vision of the seminary, it became clear that—whatever it would be—it would be "reframing" of an original vision that included academics and ministry preparation, scholarship and technological innovation. This recovery and reframing of Fuller's original vision led us to commit to being a seminary that offers the very best academic research and graduate-level scholarship as well as innovating with a digital platform that would enable us to make resources that could serve Christian leaders and organizations around the world. This new direction of serving both graduate students and learners and leaders who needed our scholarship but not a formal course of study was discerned by recovering our oldest organizational values.

For Chip Heath and Dan Heath, reframing is critical to leading change because it helps both the leaders and followers sense the *momentum* of the change process and reaffirm with every decision how enduring through the change process is a reaffirmation of one's individual and organizational *identity*. Those two factors (momentum and identity) are powerful because they deploy both the *elephant* and the *rider* at the same time. In their book *Switch*, the Heaths employ the concepts first developed by Nobel Prize–winning psychologist Daniel Kahneman and his colleague Amos Tversky, and a metaphor coined by NYU Psychologist Jonathan Haidt, to help leaders understand the psychology of change.[13]

Using the imagery of a rider (our intellect) who is directing an elephant (emotions), they illustrate how genuine, lasting change comes from using our intellect to motivate the enormous strength of our emotions. Leading change means working with both the elephant and the rider together while understanding that the elephant of emotions is much stronger, more powerful, and at times more stubbornly independent than the rational mind. In practical terms, therefore, leaders need to communicate and frame change with arguments and reasons that *inspire* and *direct* the emotions but are *supported* by rational reasons.

The Heaths identify that resilience for change is strengthened within a leader and an organization when they *feel* a sense of momentum. Earlier I mentioned the difference between a long arduous hike versus a workout on a treadmill. The treadmill is harder because of seeming lack of progress. Reframing creates the sensation of momentum. It honors an organization's past. It celebrates the progress that *has already been made* and then challenges the group to continue the work, to finish the job, to accomplish the mission that is *already in progress.*

The second reason reframing is so powerful for creating elephant resilience is that it aligns organizational change with a sense of personal and corporate *identity.* "Make change a matter of identity," the Heaths encourage. Frame change not as a departure from the identity that has been shaped through shared history and relationships but as an affirmation that the decisions and effort to bring change are deeply resonant and consistent with who we believe ourselves to be. In his speech at the Lincoln Memorial, Martin Luther King Jr. did not introduce a new idea

> *Frame change not as a departure from the identity that has been shaped through shared history and relationships but as an affirmation that the decisions and effort to bring change are deeply resonant and consistent with who we believe ourselves to be.*

for a different America but challenged the very identity of the history of America. How could it truly be the "land of the free" if a huge population of its people were not truly free?

When I do consultation work with churches, institutions, and organizations for bringing change, I always affirm that new change is a reframing of the enduring core values of the group. Adaptive change is always a healthy adaptation of the DNA, the core ideology or values, and culture of the group that is already so deeply held that to lose them would be to lose our communal identity.[14] So, when bringing change, we start *not* with dreaming about the difference the change will make in the future but with a loving gaze back to the founding and enduring stories of the group as the emotional rationale for the difference we are *called* to make. (Notice that calling or vocation is itself an *identity* statement.)

If we are facing a moment to make a change in order to make a difference in the world around us, then what of our original DNA do we bring to this moment? For Ford Motor Company it was returning to Henry Ford's original vision of cars that give the masses of people more personal freedom. For Fuller Seminary, it was the original double-vision of combining scholarship and innovation that holds to historic Christian theology while stimulating new mission and ministry around the world. In both cases, reframing inspired motivational emotions for facing resistance and accomplishing change by affirming both progress that has already been made and aligning change with an identity that is already deeply embedded and cherished.

A compelling vision—whether in a big speech or through a card with two simple words—must be framed from the organization's core identity. When it is, it recaptures and reaffirms the enduring values and taps into the cherished emotions.

When it is tenaciously repeated before an organization, it creates a commonly shared direction and at the same time the creative capacity to reorient. This reframing is a critical skill when a change process requires new creative strategies to overcome unforeseen obstacles.

CONSIDER

In what ways do your leadership practices create capacity rather than dependency in your team or community?

REORIENTING

In Silicon Valley start-up terms, nothing is scarier, more exhilarating and often more necessary than the "pivot." In start-up language, *a pivot is a change of strategy without a change of vision.*[15] A pivot occurs when a product or idea is tested and the customer data reveals that something needs to be changed for the product or idea to be more successful. On occasion the focus groups or individual customers demonstrate that the entire idea is a bad one. If that is the case, there is nothing better to learn as early as possible before investing lots of time and resources. But most of the time the feedback that comes leads to a midcourse correction, a reorientation, a new point of view that will also be tested, and if affirmed the group continues in the same direction, but further reorientation occurs if needed. Think of it like point-to-point navigation through a mountain pass with a map and a compass where we pick a waypoint and move to that one, only to then check the map and the compass before moving to the next.

Now and then we have to stop, test the map and the terrain, and keep going.

Reorienting is a leadership skill that builds resilience because it hammers in adaptability and tenacity. Reorienting requires the group to keep moving, keep aware and open to correction, and keep testing the way forward. Reorientation also fights against two common group characteristics that lead to both failure of nerve and failure of heart.

Reorienting is an answer to the inertia that comes from ambiguity. This is a paradox that takes a minute to get our heads around. When faced with the unknown of change, everything within us wants to find certainty. Certainty usually means defaulting back to the status quo. The Heaths describe this phenomenon:

> Ambiguity is exhausting to the Rider (the intellect), because the Rider is tugging on the reins of the Elephant (the emotions), trying to direct the Elephant down a new path. But when the road is uncertain, the Elephant will insist on taking the default path, the most familiar path. . . . Why? Because uncertainty makes the Elephant anxious. (Think of how, in an unfamiliar place, you gravitate toward a familiar face.) And that's why decision paralysis can be deadly for change—because the most familiar path is always the status quo.[16]

The Heaths remind us that ambiguity is the enemy of change. "Any successful change requires a translation of ambiguous goals into concrete behaviors."[17] Reorienting is a way of reducing ambiguity through learning and concrete decision making without having to have all the plans worked out perfectly and offering false promises. To reorient requires that we move *forward* in a concrete way. Moving forward means that we have to make some decisions. Every time we learn, adjust, and decide on a next step to the next waypoint, we build momentum for change. And momentum and the feelings of hope it inspires increase resilience.

LEADING RELATIONALLY

Bill Campbell, a well-known and deeply respected executive coach in Silicon Valley, was famous for his maxim "Work the team, not the problem." As former Google chairman, Eric Schmidt writes in his biography of Campbell,

> Bill didn't work the problem first, he worked the team. We didn't talk about the problem analytically. We talked about the people on the team and if they could get it done. As managers, we tend to focus on the problem at hand. What is the situation? What are the issues? What are the options? And so on. These are valid questions, but [Campbell's] instinct is to lead with a more fundamental one. Who was working on the problem? Was the right team in place? Did they have what they needed to succeed? "When I became CEO of Google," Sundar Pichai says, "Bill advised me that at that level, more than ever before, you need to bet on people. Choose your team. Think much harder about that."[18]

In his TED Talk that has been viewed over eight million times, "How to Make a Movement," Derek Sivers demonstrates how a movement starts when a lone shirtless man starts dancing all by himself at the Sasquatch! Music Festival in 2009.[19] Sivers uses a video of the dancing man, later identified as Colin Wynter, to show that the critical and often underestimated role of leadership is that of the first follower: "The first follower is what transforms a lone nut into a leader."

Sivers's point in this short video is that while a leader who starts a movement gets all the credit, what matters is that the leader treats the first followers as equals and nurtures them as people and partners. The first followers encourage others to join in (even if they remain unnamed and underappreciated), and therefore are critical to starting movements. Leaders need the validation and momentum that comes from their first followers.

The relational dynamics of leadership are unmistakable. But this is also the great challenge of leadership at the same time.

Leadership is an interdependent relationship with followers. It is one that is based on and depends on trust. Leadership requires that leaders are "easy to follow" (in Sivers' words) and that they nurture followers, but the actual challenges of the moment, the rapidly changing nature of our leadership context, the learning that we are experiencing, the losses we are preparing to face, and the adaptability needed for the demands of the decision-making cycle put us in positions where we have to make huge withdrawals from the savings account of trust, especially with our longest and most loyal followers.

Since leading change means leading people into experiences of loss, it is tempting to distance and try to simply lead by voice and vision. Further, the more attuned we are to the people we are leading, the more we begin to feel how deep the pain of change is for them. We can begin to waver in our convictions and wane in our energy for bringing change. Very often, therefore, holding *leading* and *relationship* together is difficult.

In John 6, Jesus has a large crowd, estimated at five thousand people, follow him to a mountainside to hear his teaching. He performs a miracle, feeding them all with only a few loaves of bread and fish, and the crowd is ready to "take him by force to make him king." Jesus leaves the crowd behind to go to the mountain by himself, and his disciples get in a boat to cross the sea to Capernaum. The next day (after another miracle that only the Twelve witnessed: Jesus walking on water and calming a storm), the crowds crossed the sea and joined Jesus in Capernaum.

This time, instead of feeding the crowds, Jesus challenges them to believe in him as the one who truly brings the life and light of God to the world.[20] Members of the crowd, the religious leaders who were present, enter into a debate with Jesus. Jesus continually clarifies the truth about himself in a way that is only more demanding. The debate continues into the synagogue, and the miracle worker who had fed them on the hillside the day before now comes under fire for his teaching. One day earlier the crowd had wanted to make him king, now they must face what is demanded of *them* if he is their king. Jesus would not just be the one to deliver them bread (like their ancestors ate manna in the wilderness) but would, like the God who gave their ancestors manna, require of them commitment to the saving plan of God for the world that would only come by believing and following him even to his (and possibly their own) death.

John records that the disciples begin to complain, "This teaching is difficult, who can accept it?" (v. 60). But Jesus doesn't soften his words. Following him requires belief and commitment that they must be prepared to make.

And then we read:

> Because of this many of his disciples turned back and no longer went about with him. So Jesus asked the twelve, "Do you also wish to go away?" Simon Peter answered him, "Lord, to whom can we go? You have the words of eternal life. We have come to believe and know that you are the Holy One of God." (vv. 66-69)

For all of Jesus' demanding challenges, I can't but hear the pathos of disappointment in his words to his disciples, "Do you also wish to go away?" This vignette of the ministry of Jesus reminds us of the delicate interplay between leaders and followers, of the need to build trust and prepare to disappoint the very ones who come to trust us as leaders. To meet needs and to challenge beliefs, to raise hopes and confront false expectations, to know that our leadership will be received by some and rejected by others.[21] This takes us back to sabotage and in many ways to the very worst experience of sabotage when those who have trusted us become so discouraged that they turn against us. Edwin Friedman explains,

> A major difficulty in sustaining one's mission is that others who start out with the same enthusiasm will come to lose their nerve. Mutiny and sabotage came not from enemies who opposed the initial idea, but rather from colleagues whose will was sapped by unexpected hardships along the way.[22]

Earlier I recounted the time my business administrator came to me to consider a Plan B. In the wake of the revelation that our wealthiest donor, Jay, was going to intentionally sabotage our capital building campaign, I have to admit that at that moment I was angrier at my business administrator than I was at Jay. This wasn't just a shoot-the-messenger moment on my part. I was feeling betrayed that my colleague was looking for ways to cut our losses and constrict what felt like a genuinely Spirit-led vision. But in my anger I couldn't see both my business administrator's desire for a good outcome for the church and a way of protecting me from failing. This is problematic for a leader (and one of my real weaknesses as a leader) because the lack of empathy and the presence of anger and disappointment with our colleagues tends to make them even more defensive, not less.

When we have a grounded identity focused on the development of our own resilience, then we can see others as the real human beings they are, even resisting the change that we need to make without blaming them for it. When we lead relationally from a place of understanding, then even when people are resistant to our goals and the changes we are bringing, they feel our support and safety and can begin to relax the intensity of their resistance. This relational leadership requires empathy to understand the resistance.

When I came back to Fuller to help lead the change efforts there, one of the faculty who had been my professor said to me one day, "Whatever happened to 'our' Fuller?" I could feel the pathos and longing for what theological education used to be when we had one thousand more students who were mostly residential and the campus was more abuzz with energy than it tends to be today when the majority of our students are now online. We sat for a few minutes reminiscing on the past, and over time, although I represented much of the change that my colleague resisted, we ended up working together on a significant part of the change process. Notice that I didn't change my goal, just my approach. I didn't waiver from the changes that needed to be made, I simply stayed relationally connected to my colleague while we walked through the change process. As one experienced leader told me, "When we confront resistance, if we align with the resistance instead of trying to come up against it all the time, we create the space and safety to allow the other person to finally let the resistance go."

This skill set doesn't come easy to most visionary leaders. We tend to lead by planning, enthusiasm, voice, and inspiring ideas instead of through the patient cultivating of relationships. But by learning to listen more, ask lots of questions, and develop deeper empathy with those who are feeling the loss of change, we will find that people—over time—will trust us enough to keep moving with us into the changes we need to make. This kind of relational leadership requires yet another kind of vision too.

Jim Singleton is a professor of pastoral leadership. Before moving to the seminary, Jim spent over twenty-five years as the pastor of three large churches in three different parts of the United States. Jim teaches his students that the one constant in every leadership situation is the necessity of learning to see the pain of people who are often overlooked—something his mother taught him.

> My mother was the director of Christian education in the church where I grew up. And every week over lunch after church my mother would ask me the same three questions: "Were there any new kids in Sunday school today?" I would answer, "I don't know, Mom, I was paying attention to the lesson." And then she would say, "Well, close your eyes and think back around the circle in the Sunday school class. Were there any new faces?"
>
> I would say, "Well, I guess there were. There were a couple of kids I didn't know."
>
> "Good, good," she would say. "How do you think they were feeling being new to the church and Sunday school?"
>
> I would answer, "I don't know, Mom. I can't read their minds. How am I supposed to know how they felt about being new?"
>
> She would gently chide me, "Okay, close your eyes again and think about their faces. Did they show anything that might reveal what they were feeling about being new?"
>
> I would say, "Well, one of the kids seemed to talk to the teacher a lot when he first got there. The teacher was trying to help him find a seat and feel comfortable. So maybe he wasn't so sure about being there. He may have felt uncomfortable being a new kid."
>
> "Wow, that's great that you could see that," my mother would say. "One more question: Was there anything you could have done to help them feel better about being new to the church?"

Jim continued. "This happened every week at lunch after church. Every week. My mother was the director of the Sunday school in a big church. She didn't quiz me on what I learned about the Bible, but *who* I saw who may have been having a hard day. And that formed me as a pastor. Even of large churches, learning to see and learning to have empathy for people by looking at their faces and developing empathy for their feeling made a huge difference in how I led as a pastor."[23]

LEADING UP AND SHOULDER TO SHOULDER

In Exodus 17 we find ourselves pulled into a scene rich in complexity about leading relationally. Joshua is leading a battle against Amalek, and Moses is holding high a divinely blessed staff. When his hand is raised, Joshua prevails, when Moses' hands lower, the fight begins to go against him. Moses grows weary, so some men bring him a stone to sit on. Joshua keeps fighting, but only successfully when Moses' arms are raised. Soon, Aaron and Hur join in the cause, holding up Moses' hands until the sun sets. As nightfall comes, Joshua defeats Amalek.

For Jonathan Sacks this passage is about how a leader must continually encourage the people to look to God, to maintain hope, to not despair. It is also a reminder that even the greatest leaders grow weary, and when that happens their people—especially their subordinates on the leadership team—often suffer casualties. To be Joshua on the field while Moses' arms were growing weary must have been a frightful place to be.

Perhaps the most challenging part of leading relationally for many leaders comes when they don't occupy the first chair in an organization but are responsible for a change initiative under the authority of a more senior leader.[24] Since leading change is not a function of positional authority but of functioning within any context that requires the organization, others, or ourselves to change, very often change leaders find themselves working as subordinates in a system where the senior leader is getting the majority of the resistance. And when that happens, if the senior leader begins to waver, the second-chair leader can begin to experience even more profoundly the effects of sabotage that thwarts their initiative and creativity. Edwin Friedman has a most pointed observation:

> In any type of institution whatsoever, when a self-directed, imaginative, energetic, or creative member is being consistently frustrated and sabotaged rather than encouraged and supported, what will turn out to be true one hundred percent of the time, regardless of whether the disrupters are supervisors, subordinates, or peers, is that the person at the very top of that institution is a peace-monger. By that I mean a highly anxious risk-avoider, someone who is more concerned with good feelings than with progress, someone whose life revolves around the axis of consensus.[25]

Friedman's harsh perspective should serve as a warning to first-chair leaders of how their functioning under the pressure of resistance can then cascade down and sabotage the leaders they had recruited to the team. It also helps second-chair leaders understand the dynamics that make it even more difficult to lead change when they have responsibility but incomplete authority for leading an initiative.

What then does a subordinate leader do when "consistently frustrated and sabotaged"? *Lead relationally both horizontally with peers and up the org chart.* Leading relationally does not just mean leading your people but leading with peers and leading up to one's superiors. In Exodus 17 we see this when it takes not only Joshua's military skill and Moses' divine staff but also Aaron and Hur holding Moses' arms. And this is especially critical when the senior leader begins to falter.

Experienced executive pastor, consultant, and executive coach Mike Bonem describes the importance for second-chair leaders to manage their own disappointment. Bonem counsels that if a second-chair leader believes the mission is God-given and the first chair is God's chosen person:

> Then, I think the resilient response is to stay committed to the mission and the first chair. Sure, they can and should voice concerns to the first chair in appropriate ways, but it's not OK to go rogue or to quit. This isn't resilience in the face of resistance— it's resilience in the face of frustration and discouragement.[26]

How does one do this? By staying, as much as it depends on you, as relationally connected to both allies and the senior leader, as possible. The critical component for leading relationally with a superior (especially a superior who can become a peace monger) is to focus on having a good, clear, trusting relationship. Very often when a senior leader is faltering, the first sign is that they begin to distance from the team. The failure of nerve internally leads to a failure of heart relationally. The more that junior leaders can be like Joshua, who is faithfully leading by moving the strategy ahead, and Aaron and Hur, who are helping to bolster the senior leader, the more likely the change initiative will succeed. Leading relationally means leading as a team and together holding both the initiative for the change and the morale for the group. Sacks describes it this way:

> A fundamental principle of leadership is being taught here. A leader must empower the team. He cannot do the work for them; they must do it for themselves. But he must, at the same time, give them the absolute confidence that they can do it and succeed. The leader is responsible for their mood and morale. During the battle, he must betray no sign of weakness, doubt, or fear. That is not always easy. Moses' hands "became weary." All leaders have their moments of exhaustion. At such times the leader needs support—even Moses needed the help of Aaron

and Hur. In the end, though, his upraised hands were the sign the Israelites needed that God was giving them the strength to prevail, and they did.[27]

In my own leadership I have played the role of every character in this vignette. I have been the subordinate, Joshua, leading the charge, the supportive Aaron and Hur who are encouraging the leader, and the weary Moses. And never was leading relationally with empathy and connection and shared goals more important than when I was in the middle of sabotage with disgruntled member Jay and my wavering business administrator asking about Plan B for our capital campaign.

BACK TO THE SABOTAGE IN THE SANCTUARY

After the whole story came out about Jay's hurt feelings and his plan to have his friends all give small checks to the capital campaign, I took a deep breath and asked a trusted leader to join the business administrator and me in a conversation about what we should do. While we didn't know the mantra of the Lombard Mennonite Peace Center at the time, our strategy for dealing with the sabotage was the same. "Stay calm, stay connected and stay the course" could be the playbook for what we did.[28]

At least *this* time I let my emotions fade (stay calm) and began to see that my business administrator was trying to be Aaron and support me. He wasn't second-guessing the decision as much as he was trying to make sure I was aware of what we were facing so he could help me. Since Jay was a private and proud man who would likely not have taken well to a young, new pastor even knowing his comments, letting alone talking to him about them, I went against my usual practice of trying to talk through conflict and decided to wait until Jay raised the subject. We also decided that other leaders in the church who were closer in age and respected by Jay would intentionally *stay connected* to him.

And without question there was no Plan B. We were committed to staying the course. We would continue with the capital campaign trusting that God had led us to this decision and that God would provide what we needed. We also decided that staying the course meant there would be no expectation that Jay or his friends would ever participate in giving to the campaign. They were members of the church and had every right and should have every expectation that they could receive the fellowship, spiritual support, and pastoral care they had always received. There was no rule that to be a member in good standing one needed to like the pastor and give to the capital campaign. They would be treated the same and would be honored and cared for as the long-time members of the church they were.

And when the totals of money pledged and received came in from the capital campaign, we had everything we needed to continue with the building project. Jay didn't give a big gift to the campaign. God just provided through others. And to my knowledge Jay never gave us a significant amount of money again. In staying the course, we didn't let the anxious sabotage of a hurt man and a blundering pastor stop what God wanted to accomplish.

To be sure, Jay was mad at me for a long time. He barely spoke to me and communicated his displeasure in a most interesting way. Jay's hobby was hand carving ducks out of wood. He was an avid duck hunter and skilled carver. And he would make a beautiful duck and then give it to someone as a sign of affection and respect. Over time, all of the pastors and the staff received ducks from Jay. All, that is, except me.

But as the years went by and as he stayed within the congregation, our associate pastor mostly kept connected to him—especially when he was diagnosed with cancer. Our congregation rallied around Jay and loved him. They supported his wife, and no one ever said a word about the capital campaign or the things he'd said. He was just one of our own.

One day there was a knock at the door: Jay was there. He asked to speak with me, and we talked about how his life was coming to an end soon. He asked me to share in officiating his memorial service when the time came and as he left—he gave me a carved duck. Inscribed, "To my friend and Pastor Tod."

Leading change is not just about what happens in the organization. Yes, the buildings were built and the campus was renovated and the church became more outward focused and more engaged in the community. It took nine years, but as the place was transformed, so were we. Adaptive leadership, we must remember, is as much about the transformation of the people who go through the change process as it is about the change. Including a hurt man and a blundering pastor who—eventually—became friends.

8

TEMPERING

RESILIENCE COMES THROUGH A RHYTHM OF LEADING AND NOT LEADING

> *Two chisels on an anvil-maybe...*
> *Take these two chisel-pals, O God*
> *Take 'em and beat 'em, hammer 'em, hear 'em laugh.*
>
> CARL SANDBURG, *LAUGHING BLUE STEEL*

> *Today of course I still assess the quality of my work.*
> *But I also ask myself a whole other set of questions about my*
> *life. Did I devote enough time to my family? Did I learn enough*
> *new things? Did I develop new friendships and deepen old*
> *ones? These would have been laughable to me when I was*
> *25, but as I get older, they are much more meaningful.*
>
> BILL GATES

THE OLD PASTOR WALKED UP TO ME as I finished my last presentation in a retreat center outside of Cleveland, Ohio. His muscular frame was betrayed by a limp; his thick face softened by a kindly smile.

"I love hearing you talk about tempering a tool. It takes me back," he said. "Many years ago, before I was a pastor, I was a miner in West Virginia. At the end of the day, no matter how long we had been down in that mine, we couldn't go home until we tempered our picks. Every day, at the end of the day, we had to take our picks to the forge and slowly heat it, file it for tomorrow, and then heat it again and let it cool. We would keep doing that process until a blue line ran down the middle of the steel head of the pick. Once it was blue, we could go home because our pick was ready for the next day."

What does it take to be ready for the next day of leading? What does it take to become a tool that has the resilience to be used by God to hew stones of hope out of a mountain of despair. and to keep doing so day after day, year after year? If the work of using a tool adds stress to the tool and that stress both strengthens it and hardens it, it would seem that the key to making a tool that is resilient in the face of resistance would mostly require that we just keep using it. And if we are that tool, then we should just keep chipping away at the challenges and obstacles that face us, trusting that we will become stronger and tougher the more energy and effort we put into it.

> *What does it take to be ready for the next day of leading? What does it take to become a tool that has the resilience to be used by God to hew stones of hope out of a mountain of despair. and to keep doing so day after day, year after year?*

Or will we? I learned from blacksmiths that if we want a tool to become tempered there is a process of stress and rest, of heating the steel and letting it cool, of using the tool and releasing the stress that needs to become the regular rhythm of the tool.

BECOMING A TEMPERED LEADER

Working: Leaders are formed in leading.

Heating: Strength is forged in self-reflection.

Holding: Vulnerable leadership requires relational security.

Hammering: Stress makes a leader.

Hewing: Resilience takes practice.

Tempering: Resilience comes through a rhythm of leading and not leading.

In metallurgy, tempering is a heat treatment that *includes* heating the tool and shaping it at very high heat on an anvil, using tools, and then plunging it into the water to cool it. That plunging hardens the tool, locking the stress into the tool, making it a stronger piece of steel.

But if you used the tool right then, with all of the stress in it, it would likely soon become too brittle, the steel holding too much stress. It needs instead to be cooled, slowly heated up again, and slowly cooled again until it reaches the proper level of what metallurgists call the critical point, that is the place where hardness and flexibility exist for the tool to do its job.[1]

Throughout this book we have been learning that resilience comes from the stress that creates strength. At the same time, too much stress means that both steel and leaders become brittle instruments that crumble beneath the task. This is the delicate balance. For the tool to remain both resilient and useful, it cannot be just strong; it has to be tempered. It has to be quenched or cooled slowly. Tempering takes the stress out of the tool by reheating and slowly cooling. When a tool is tempered, the excess stress is removed, *toughness* is increased, and brittleness is decreased at the same time.

If the leader's failure of nerve can be attributed to being too soft and too compliant with the anxiety of the system, failure of heart is the outcome of a leader that has become discouraged, emotionally disconnected, and too brittle. A *rhythm* of stress and rest tempers a tool and builds in the strength and flexibility that bring resilience. As two researchers concluded, "The key to resilience is trying really hard, then stopping, recovering, and then trying again."[2]

> *Resilience comes from stress that creates strength. At the same time, too much stress means that both steel and leaders become brittle instruments that crumble beneath the task. This is the delicate balance.*

Tempering, again, is not a one-time plunge into a cold pool or a once-a-year vacation or retreat. It is a regular, repetitive process: The heat of the crucible of leadership is only intensified through reflection. The same hammering of spiritual practices is only intensified through the practice of leadership. Both shaping the leader into a tool and the use of the tool is intense and hammers in stress in the leader. But, in both shaping and leading, the actual *tempering* occurs during times of cooling or quenching, slowly releasing leadership responsibilities at least temporarily.

This rhythm is the process for a tempered leader: *heating* through work and reflection, *holding* of good relationships both personally and professionally, the *hammering* of spiritual practices and the practice of leadership, and the *tempering* that comes through cooling periods of rest and release from leading, and then repeated (see fig. 8.1). Like the old miner and his pick with the blue line, we are not ready for the next leadership task until we are tempered.

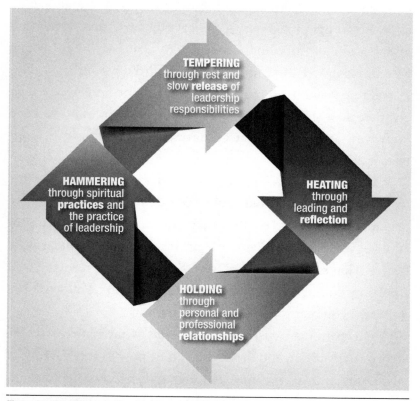

Figure 8.1. The process for forming tempered resilience

This pattern has also been the key insight for training world-class athletes for half a century. Bill Bowerman was the legendary track coach from the University of Oregon in the 1950s and 1960s. As a coach he was to running what UCLA's John Wooden was to college basketball. But even more than that, he is credited with having convinced ordinary people that they should take up jogging for exercise. (Before him, most people would have felt and looked a little silly going for a run for no reason unless they were competitive athletes.)

Bowerman was an innovator in lots of ways. Indeed, it was Bowerman's genius that led to the modern running shoe; he used his wife's waffle iron to create the first wide rubber-soled shoe. He brought jogging to America after a trip to New Zealand and was one of the cofounders of Nike.[3] And he was the coach who popularized alternating between hard days and easy days in training, saying, on hard days go hard but on easy days go easy. He said that athletes need a rhythm of training to keep improving and that they can't improve by doing the same things over and over again.

At the beginning of the season he used to gather his recruits to the university and tell them, "Gentleman, take a primitive organism, any weak, pitiful organism. Make it lift or jump or run. Let it rest. What happens? A little miracle. It gets a little better. That's all training is. Stress—recover—improve. You'd think any damn fool could do it. . . . But you don't. You work too hard and you rest too little and you get hurt."[4]

When exercise physiologists discuss what it takes to get stronger, healthier, and fitter, they point now to this rhythm of stretching and resting, of extending and then pulling back. In other words, if all we do is the same twenty-minute walk, then we'll never get any fitter than what it takes to do a twenty-minute walk with more efficiency. But when we create a rhythm of adding more time or intensity *and* then more time to recover, we will grow stronger and fitter.

Without even recognizing it Bowerman was pointing to the rhythm for living the way God intended. *Stress, recover, improve.* And the problem with most of us is that we do *neither* stressing nor recovering—we just keep doing the same things that keep us comfortable and reinforce what we are already doing. Without both a rhythm of stress *and* rest—of heating and quenching—we will never become both stronger and more flexible, both tougher and healthier. As important as the work of leading is, it is the moments of *not* leading that tempers the resilient leader.

> *"The key to resilience is trying really hard, then stopping, recovering, and then trying again."*

So, what does that rhythm look like in the life of a leader? Because I am a Christian leader, it is a process that begins with also remembering that my priority is not to be a leader but a *worshiper*. Worship, not work; honoring and dedicating myself to God and not leading—even in God's name—is the first priority of every week.

WORK AND WORSHIP, LEADING AND NOT LEADING

An older friend and mentor sent me a text message one Sunday morning when I was away from the seminary for a few weeks to finish writing this book. "I prayed for you this morning. How are you feeling about glorifying God in your ministry?"

The message took me back to my old friend and mentor, Al, who has since passed away. He used to send me handmade postcards through the US mail. They would show up at the seminary office with a simple note. "I'm praying for you; what are *you* doing for God's kingdom *today*?"

These two friends, two mentors, both wise Christians who had been successful business leaders, have been important voices in my life. They pray, they have supported me, and they often reminded me regularly that my work has a purpose, a focus, a reason for being: glorify God, extend God's love, grace, and justice of the reign of God in the world.

The recent Sunday morning when I received the text message about glorifying God, I found myself reflecting on the question: *Am I?* Is my work at the seminary, my speaking, and my writing revealing God's presence to the world? Is my ministry glorifying God? My honest answer is twofold: (1) I hope so, and (2) I could do more.

My temptation when I receive such a nudge is to get back to work as soon as I can. To put my head down and to try to accomplish as much as I can for God on this particular day, to roll up my sleeves and do something that will glorify God and extend his reign of grace, love, and justice.

But it was Sunday. It was the sabbath day. And on the sabbath the point of the day is not working but *ceasing,* not doing more but enjoying the work of our hands and reflecting deeper on the God who gives us a good life to live and good work to do.[5] The point of the text that morning from my friend was not to prepare me for work but for *worship.*

In worship that morning the guest pastor was another older friend and mentor (I was beginning to see a pattern). He preached on Ecclesiastes 3, the famous "For everything there is a season, and a time for every matter under heaven" passage that includes

a time to plant, and a time to pluck up what is planted . . .
a time to break down, and a time to build up . . .
a time to throw away stones, and a time to gather stones
together. (vv. 2-3, 5)

And then in the middle of the next passage were these verses:

What gain have the workers from their toil? . . . I know that there is nothing better for them than to be happy and enjoy themselves as long as they live; moreover, it is God's gift that all should eat and drink and take pleasure in all their toil. I know that whatever God does endures forever; nothing can be added to it, nor anything taken from it; God has done this, so that all should stand in awe before him. (vv. 9, 12-14)

Commentators on this passage often take the author's tone as one of cynical resignation: the world turns, nothing changes, we will all live and die, so we should just eat and drink and enjoy our work. Only what God does lasts, we humans should just eat and drink and enjoy our work. But that tone misses the critical point of the passage to me. *If* all there is in this world is what we can see, and if it is impossible to know if our work will endure, then, yes, "eat, drink, enjoy your work." But *if instead* we can align our work and our lives to the work and life of God, which *will endure*, then "eating, drinking and working" become gifts of God and a good *rhythm* for living.

Only what *God* does endures forever, the preacher of Ecclesiastes reminds us, and that should cause us to worship God ("stand in awe before him"). But if the very purpose of our work and our leadership is to align our work with God's work, to express in the work of leadership that the changes we are laboring to bring are to help align the world with God's will so God's will be revealed and glorified, then how shall we work? How shall we *live*? How shall we *lead*?

This truth—that my life and leadership is to reveal God's work in the world ("glorify God")—is the daily reminder that my work is to align with God's work. My will is to be aligned with God's will. And my leadership is to always be about the kinds of changes that God is bringing into the world. Even the *way* of leading is to be aligned with God's way of working. And even God enjoyed the sabbath.

Genesis tells us that even God ceased working on the sabbath. The picture of Genesis 3 is not of a tired God who needed a day off (how does an omnipotent Being tire?) but of a joyful God "walking in the garden at the time of the evening breeze." You can almost picture God wanting to take a stroll with his children, simply taking in and enjoying creation.

With this image of God in mind, see the beautiful restorative rhythm that is a gift of God, "it is God's gift that all should eat and drink and take pleasure in all their toil" (v. 13). Good work that is pleasurable and meaningful. Good walks in creation, good meals, surrounded by loved ones that remind us of God's generosity and grace in our lives. Good work, enjoyment, meals with family and friends.

When I received the text from my friend that Sunday morning, I was tempted to want to do more for God. But my friend wrote on a Sunday, and I was heading to worship, and that is really what I needed. I needed the rhythm of not working that day, of not leading that morning, of not doing anything *for* God, and instead showing up and being *with* God.

My postcard-writing friend, Al, was the husband in the anvil-anchoring couple who dedicated themselves to give us a "great ministry and a great life." They had grown up on a farm in Iowa. They understood a lot about the rhythms of living.

That Sunday after the text message and the sermon on Ecclesiastes, Beth and I returned to our little place in Idaho where we were spending the month so I could write. She took a nap, I made soup from the barbecued chicken leftover from dinner the night before. As the soup simmered in the slow cooker, we took a hike along a small creek in an aspen forest. We talked about the worship service that morning and about our adult kids who are busy with jobs and relationships and whom we especially miss at Sunday dinners. We talked a little about my book and her art and what we were learning about ourselves. But mostly we just took in the beauty of the evening breeze. We returned home to the soup and an evening together and calls and text messages with our adult kids. And the next day we would get back to work.

This rhythm of working and not working, leading and not leading, toiling and enjoying, being diligent and being thankful, of good ministry and good life creates both a resilient leader and a healthy community.

For me this same pattern makes up the rhythm of our sabbath rituals now that I am not a pastor. One of the practices of our Sunday is to continue the family tradition of Sunday dinners—cooking, some time spent outside, a good nap. And now, since I left the pastorate to work at a seminary, it includes being slightly *late* to worship.

For years when I was pastoring, I led between two and four services a Sunday. Beth used to show up faithfully for the 11 a.m. service every week. The only problem, in my opinion, was that the service started at 10:45! Usually, after church I would needle Beth about how she is late to worship every week. She would take my teasing and remind me that she often saw people from the earlier service on the patio, so she would stop and chat. And, yes, she usually ran about five minutes behind. Besides, she would tease me back, she only missed the announcements and she had me at home to remind her of anything that was coming up at church.

After I left the pastorate, Beth and I were able to attend worship together. This was a great gift after twenty-seven years of marriage when during worship I sat up front and she sat with our kids and our friends. But this also brought to a head the differences in our punctuality for worship. After over two decades of leading worship services, I was trained for being on time—even early. But Beth was used to a more fluid sense of what *on time* was.

One morning, as we were late *again*, I was seething. We finally took our place in the pew and I apologized to the people we stepped over for interrupting their worship. My mind was racing and I was distracted in prayer. I was irritated at Beth and was already thinking of what I was going to say to her after church that would help her see how rude it was that we were late all of the time. However, I was not focusing my attention on the gift of worshiping God alongside my wife.

And in the silence I felt like God said to me, "Whenever you are late to worship, let it be a reminder to you that you are *not* leading this service. The pastor is doing a great job. He doesn't need you to be on time. You need to attend worship with Beth and let the worship team and the pastor lead *you*. Let your spiritual practice *not* be about caring what time you arrive for worship but enjoying worshiping with Beth."

I needed to be reminded that as someone who is often leading, this was *not* where I was called to lead. Worship is the place where I am called to follow, and worshiping with Beth with a nonjudgmental heart was more important for what I needed in my life than to be there on time.

So now, at least one of my spiritual practices, is being—at least a little bit—*late* to worship.

CONSIDER

What are the most restorative acts that are part of your life? Are they valuable enough to you to make them a regular rhythm of your life of leadership?

AIRPORT TOD GOES TO IDAHO

A regular rhythm of leading and not leading, including a commitment to sabbath worship, Sunday dinners, and even being late to church, is part of the regular tempering rhythm of my life and leadership. But an even more powerful tempering practice is often mentioned in leadership literature and seen most profoundly in the life and leadership of Jesus: retreating from leading and into nature.

Jesus started his ministry with forty days of preparation in the wilderness. A personal season of connection and encounter with God, his forty days mirror Israel's own forty years in the wilderness between the exodus and the Promised Land. It is also a time when Jesus faced temptations and experienced the ministry of the angels (Matthew 4).

Because leading change is stressful for me, I must prioritize rest and recreation, sleeping deeply and having long meals with friends, praying and playing. Specifically, it is best expressed through building into my rule of life a commitment to a regular personal retreat. While for many years I would do this through the generosity of friends or in simple hiking, camping, or backpacking trips, I am blessed in this season of my life to have a small mountain home in Idaho, where I can immerse myself in nature, "sauntering," as John Muir called it, walking slowly (or often fly-fishing slowly) through God's creation like a pilgrim in the Holy Land.[6]

My family likes to tease me that when I travel for work I turn into "Airport Tod." Airport Tod is efficient down to the minute, knows exactly how to navigate both Los Angeles traffic and the always crowded LAX airport. I have both Clear and TSA Pre so I can whisk my way through the security lines, I know how to spy who is going to slow down the line and speed up my step to get in front. I walk at a pace that makes sure nothing impedes getting to my gate in time to make sure that I—and my carry-on bag—both get on without a problem. I'm efficient, focused, and truth be told a bit *too* driven.

One day my wife and my daughter were traveling with me to our place in Idaho for a few days of relaxation. Both Beth and Ali started laughing at me and teasing me to slow down as I cut off a lady with a walker to make sure that I got in front of her in the security line. It may have been a leisure trip, but I had defaulted into driven, goal-oriented Airport-Tod mode just to get *to* our place.

I *love* our place in Idaho. It is an enormous grace in my life. It's where I go to rest, to sleep, to pray, to play. It's where I hike and fish in the summer and make roaring fires in the winter. It's where I cook meals and read and watch movies until late into the evening. When I am with my friends and family having a meal outside in a beautiful place, I can feel my soul being strengthened and my heart being softened in gratitude. When my adult children are home, I can barely make it through grace without weeping. When we are in our little place eating on our deck and looking at the Idaho Smoky Mountains, I feel like God is lavishing on me what I need to restore myself to the work that the Spirit has called me to do.

And soon I am breathing deeply, walking slowly, *sauntering* on wooded trails, smiling a relaxed smile. Sitting outside one afternoon eating a tuna sandwich at a picnic table, my daughter noticed how rested I had become. "Dad," she said, "I have to admit, I like *Idaho Tod* a lot better than Airport Tod."

I have found that the heavier the demands of leading, the more regularly I should take both brief moments or longer stretches to leave behind the leading; to take a walk outside, sit on the sidelines, and observe; to rest and reflect and remind myself that I am loved before I do anything—and then like a miner's pick that has turned a good-tempered blue, I'm ready to enter back into the work again.

RETURNING TO HEWING

On that hot August day in 1963, Dr. King stood on the steps of the Lincoln Memorial before a throng of people who knew the cost and the long road of trying to bring genuine, deep, and lasting change to a society stuck in the injustice of the status quo. His voice cried out and his rhetoric soared. He spoke of a vision of a new day—and of going back to the task.

Hewing hope from despair is hard work. It's not something that just happens. Transforming discord into a beautiful symphony takes deliberate, diligent, and dedicated people. Leading adaptive change requires more from us than we can muster with our good intentions. It requires forging.

A tempered leader is formed in the crucible of leading through reflection, relationships, and a rule of life in a rhythm of leading and not leading.

A tempered leader has resilience formed through a grounded identity, and teachable, attuned, adaptable, and tenacious character.

A tempered leader hammers resilience into people through managing reactivity, reframing, reorienting, and leading relationally.

And like a tempered tool that has been made stronger and more flexible than the raw material alone, the leader often needs to be sharpened, honed, and reforged again and again. And again.

WHY IS THIS SO HARD?

*"It's a simple way of farming." That's what Alan always says.
It's just not easy. In his own way, I think he's
always been honest with us about that.*

THE BIGGEST LITTLE FARM IN THE WORLD

THE WOMAN SITTING ACROSS THE TABLE from me was as experienced working closely with leaders as anyone I have ever met. A trained marriage and family therapist, a certified spiritual director, an experienced executive coach, she is a master at using tools like StrengthsFinder, the Enneagram, and the Ignatian *Spiritual Exercises.* She has listened to, consulted with, and engaged the deepest fears and insecurities, the daily demands and tricky nuances of leaders in diversely different contexts. So, when she raised her question, it took me aback: "I am not sure there are many people who can actually lead the kind of change you are talking about. Most leaders I know can't. And to be frank, even more will say that it isn't worth it."

I listened as she continued, asking, "Why should anyone work so hard to face such resistance for so long?"

I swallowed hard and took a deep breath. It's almost like she was describing the details of the mountain of despair, and she was echoing the words of so many leaders I have met over the years.

My answer to the first part of her comment is all that you have read so far.

- Leading change is difficult. It requires us to hew hope out of despair.

- Becoming a tempered leader is the way to become the chisel that God can use to bring transformation out of the mountains of resistance that leaders face.

- It takes a resilient, tempered leader to develop the resilient, adaptive capacity of a community, group, organization, institution, or congregation.

But as to her other question—the *why* question—well, that's the most important thing of all. And it takes us back to the board room in Silicon Valley: *Why should we even do this?*

THE WHY OF LEADERSHIP

Simon Sinek has made a name for himself making one point: "People don't buy what you do, they buy *why* you do it." His TED Talk, "How Great Leaders Inspire Action," has been viewed over 45 million times. Sinek lays out his view that the key to bringing change is to "start with 'why.'" While his premise has given rise to a chicken-egg debate, what is clear is that inner motivation or purpose is directly linked to motivating others to buy in to a plan.

In the talk he draws a diagram of three circles; the center circle is labeled "why" and two outer rings are labeled "what" and "how." "People don't buy what you do, they buy why you do it," he repeats. The motivation for changing behavior and bringing change to the world is not in the strategies (the *what*) or the tactics (the *how*) but in the motivation (the *why*). For Sinek the driver of change is to find those people who share *at the center of their being* your same central beliefs and motivations and engage them in joining you.

Leadership is born not of the desire to lead but—at the center of our being—out of *a call to service in light of the brutal facts of the world.* It flows not from a desire to achieve, succeed, or accomplish, but to *serve* at the point of real need and experiencing that need as one's own calling.[1]

Leadership expert Marty Linsky says in an interview with *Faith and Leadership,* "People who are willing to take the risks of exercising leadership do so *on behalf of something they care deeply about.*"[2] In other words, there must be a compelling *why* for leading that is about a genuine need in the world.

Christian leadership that flows from the center of our being must begin in aligning our motivations with the purposes of God; the intentions and activities we see in the Scriptures come from the center of *Jesus'* being—the things God deeply cares about (John 1:18). In his book *The Jesus Creed,* New Testament scholar Scot McKnight writes about Jesus' most audacious and innovative mash-up of the commands of God. These two lines, writes McKnight, are the starting point for any spiritual formation and the key to understanding the unique adaptation that Jesus' presence brings to the revelation of God given to Israel.[3] For McKnight, Jesus' teaching leads to the "first amendment" to the fundamental commandment given to God's people. And it was both a scandal and an act of leadership that demands our attention if we too are going to lead others into the mission of God in the world. But let's start with this thought experiment.

Imagine that you are standing in church and reciting the Apostles' Creed in unison. Like believers have done for centuries, you are speaking aloud that great old creed that serves as the synopsis of what a person has to believe and affirm in order to be a Christian. Indeed, in many circles this includes the core doctrines we must confess without our fingers crossed. It is considered *essential*.

Imagine that you are in your church standing together, the words on a screen in front of you, and in one voice you declare, "I believe in God the Father Almighty. . . . I believe in Jesus Christ his only Son our Lord. . . . I believe in the Holy Spirit. I believe in the Holy Catholic Church." In its succinctness it builds to a crescendo: "I believe in the resurrection of the body and life everlasting!" and just when you are ready to add a hearty "Amen," one more slide appears and says, "And that every person should tithe to the local church!" or "That every Christian will share the gospel with friends and neighbors!" Or "That every Christian will work for justice!"

What would you think? You may agree wholeheartedly with these statements, but something would seem seriously wrong, right? These are good ideas, but you don't mess with the creed. You just don't add things to the "essentials of belief."

But this is exactly what Jesus does.

> When the Pharisees heard that he had silenced the Sadducees, they gathered together, and one of them, a lawyer, asked him a question to test him. "Teacher, which commandment in the law is the greatest?" He said to him, "You shall love the Lord your God with all your heart, and with all your soul, and with all your mind." This is the greatest and first commandment. (Matthew 22:34-38)

I believe that at this moment, the faces of the religious leaders would have been beaming in smiles. *The young rabbi knows his stuff*, they would have been thinking. He just quoted the beginning of the Shema of Deuteronomy 6:5, the basic teaching, the core commandment, the closest thing to a creed that the

Jews had. And it is worth pausing here to note that if Jesus would have stopped right here, all would have probably been well with those Pharisees. He would very likely have passed their test. Indeed, I believe that if he would have stopped there, he might even have avoided crucifixion.

But he didn't stop there. With barely a breath he heads into the rest of his answer: "And a second is like it: 'You shall love your neighbor as yourself.' On these two commandments hang all the law and the prophets" (vv. 39-40).

What? The Pharisees would have been asking, shocked by what they have heard. *What did he say?* This may have been the issue that made the Pharisees turn on him. But why? Jesus didn't just make up his own teaching here. He quotes from Leviticus. It's a biblical statement, a statement from the Torah. So, what could be the problem?

When Christians recite the Apostles' Creed, it is very similar to Jews reciting the Shema. And you don't take good things, even really good things, and make them essential things. Only what is essential must be essential. And this is exactly what Jesus does. He makes a really good thing—a really important thing, even a good and important biblical thing—an *essential* thing. Something that is required of everyone who would be his followers.

And that changes *everything*.

Jesus says to them: "It is not enough to love God. It's not enough to know God personally, have faith and confidence in God's love for you. It's not enough to be spiritual. It's not enough to be religious, to go to church, to live for a higher power. It's also not enough to have a good church, a healthy church, a growing church. Those things are good but they are not enough."

The end or goal of life for Jesus—whether for an individual or a community—is to love God *and* love others. *And they are equal in importance.* You cannot have one without the other. You must, must, must have both. Jesus says that to live with the ultimate end in mind, to live out the greatest commandment, to live in a way that pleases God is *not just to love God but also to love the world the way God so loves it.*[4]

It is this conviction that forms the *why* of leadership. For followers of Jesus there is nothing we are called to care about as much as the love and justice of God reaching our neighbor and being expressed in all of creation. In theological terms, the venture capitalist I made my innovation pitch to in Silicon Valley was challenging the seminary professor about the most basic question asked of Jesus: "Who is my neighbor?"

CONSIDER
What is your own, personal, compelling why for leadership? Why do you work so hard to bring change?

GIVING UP ON THE WORK OR GIVING THE WORK BACK?

Considering this larger *why* of leadership also brings us squarely to the single most delicate issue of dealing with resistance and developing resilience. When do we know it's time to walk away or give up on the effort to bring change? Or to put it another way: *Is moving on from a change leadership process a sign of the failure to develop resilience?*

To answer this delicate question, we need to be clear about two key truths:

Most change initiatives fail. People stubbornly and profoundly resist change. Alan Deutschman discovered in his research about people who were told by their doctors that they needed to change their lives or they would die, 90 percent would choose to risk death rather than change.[5] Seventy-five percent of venture-capital-backed Silicon Valley start-ups fail.[6] Seventy percent of *all* organizational change efforts also fail.[7] This work is very difficult, and the calling to do so requires that we see ourselves as participating in something much greater and more important than the survival or fruitfulness of any particular organization, congregation, or institution.

Success or failure in leading change is as much about what happens in the lives of the people as what happens in the organization. The long-term fruitfulness is people who grow in their adaptive capacity to become lifelong learners who learn to navigate necessary losses with hope and courage. These leaders, formed to be used by God, will also encourage genuine transformation wherever they go. The development of people with the capacity to hew hope out of despair and transform discord into harmonious communities—wherever they are—is more important than any one change effort.

Which requires us to be clear about a second truth.

Adaptive change only occurs when the work is "given back to the people." If leading change in a Christian context means that all effort and energy is as much about the transformation of the people in the change process as it is the organization or institution you are endeavoring to change, then *that* clarifies our ultimate challenge. Adaptive change does not come because a great leader solves a hard problem with resolve and a clear plan. Adaptive change comes because the community, the group, the team, the institution, the organization, the congregation take responsibility for their transformation and begin to change. Only when the people who must change begin to see the challenges of a changing world as *their* problem not the leaders' problem does change occur. And that change must be a genuine transformation. As Heifetz writes, "To meet adaptive challenges, people must change their hearts as well as their behaviors."[8]

So, what do these two truths tell us about when to know if it's time to walk away from a change process? They remind us that it is not a lack of resilience to know—that since it is normal and natural for people facing the hard work of changing to give up—when the people themselves refuse to take on the work of changing, then your season as a change leader is over.

This is not something that we come to lightly. It's not about walking away at the earliest sign (or even multiple signs) of resistance. But it does mean that a day *will very likely come* when no matter what you do, your change efforts in this instance will cease and you will have to walk away and discern for yourself what to do next.

What do tempered, resilient change leaders do when they walk away from a group that didn't change? They find a new group and start a new change process. Why? Because as long as there is need for groups who will fulfill the charge to love our neighbor, and as long as there is need for hope amidst despair, and as long as there is longing to hear the "jangling discords" turn into "symphony" of fellowship, there remains the need for people to function as leaders.

This, Jonathan Sacks reminds us, is worthy of a long process of transformation.

> "It is not for you to complete the task, but neither are you free to desist from it" (Mishna Avot 2:16). Leadership involves a delicate balance between impatience and patience. Go too fast and people resist. Go too slow and they become complacent. Transformation takes time, often more than a single generation.[9]

And perhaps that's the most important lesson of all.

To participate in the kinds of change that will make the world (or even our little corner of the world) what it is supposed to be is a work worthy of our entire lives—and will often take more than one lifetime to do so.

That is work that requires resilience.

What could be more meaningful than that?

ACKNOWLEDGMENTS

*T*HIS BOOK IS THE FRUIT OF CONVERSATION. Honest, rich, vulnerable conversation.

Very often over the past five years when I was asked to speak to a group of leaders on adaptive change, the most important meeting was not the one where I was speaking, but where I was listening; it was not during the plenary but at a meal with my hosts and a few colleagues. It was in those relaxed gatherings that I heard most deeply the deep commitment to lead well and the dear cost from facing resistance. Those dinners became both confessionals and coaching sessions, both opportunities to share stories from the floor and observations from the balcony.

As those conversations continued in very different contexts—in a pub outside of Edinburgh, at a dinner with longtime friends in Georgia, over sushi in New York City, in a hotel lobby in Toronto, over cocktails in Grand Rapids, in a diner in Louisville, in a neighborhood café in Auckland, in countless church halls and hotel conference rooms, with my students, with my coaching clients, in interviews with experienced leaders, and in many conversations around my own dinner table—I heard such similar themes that it made me realize that there was a particular work to be done.

At the same time, I was also writing this book during a season of immense change and challenge in my own institution as part of a massive—and as yet unfinished—organizational change effort. I have lived everything that I have written. Failures of nerve and failures of heart are very familiar to me.

So this book could not have been written without the voices of well over a hundred different leaders from around the world. In addition, my doctor of ministry students helped me work on and work out all of these concepts both in the classroom and in their own places of leadership. To all of them who invited me into their leadership work and allowed me to walk with them for a few steps in the change journey, I offer my humble thanks.

This was also shaped by conversations with colleagues and friends who read portions of the manuscript and gave me the kind of candid feedback that only comes through a shared passion for the outcome. I want to especially thank Lynn Ziegenfuss, Mark Roberts, Linda Roberts, Mary Andringa, Dale Andringa, Jim Singleton, Laura Murray, Matthew Colwell, Daniel White, Jeff Hoffmeyer, Corey Widmer, Jack Peebles, Thomas Daniel, Andre Henry, Theresa Cho, Kevass Harding, Michelle Louis, Steve Yamaguchi, John Chandler, Charlie Campbell, Terry Looper, and Mark Labberton for the gift of their encouragement and experience. The book is much stronger because of your care and candor. To that list of contributors and wise voices, I have to also add my gratitude to my agent, Kathryn Helmers, and to IVP and especially my editor, Cindy Bunch. Both of you make me a stronger writer, and I am in your debt.

I have benefited from a team at Fuller that is so good at what they do that I am able to travel, think, write and engage the broader church, but I have to especially thank Angela Bae for her extraordinary capacity to keep the work on task when I am literally or figuratively in the clouds.

Let me also add my thanks to Heather McClarty of Adam's Forge in Los Angeles for giving me a tour of her outdoor artisan blacksmithing shop and answering all of my questions on blacksmithing.

Anyone who has read this far knows that the most tender, treasured, and transformative part of the crucible of change is when a vulnerable leader experiences the security of the anvil. I write about it from my own experience. So, to my own anvil of colleagues, friends, and family members who have held me as I continue to be shaped as a leader, I add my deepest thanks: Beth, Brooks, Ali and Ben—you know that I literally can't live or lead without you. Linda and Mark, Charlie and Tracy, Rob and Elizabeth, Mike and Steph—the joy of meals and years of friendship is a more cherished gift each day. Steve Yamaguchi, Lynn Ziegenfuss, and Terry Looper—you are friends and mentors that I have needed more often than you know.

To all of you, thanks for holding me so well.

This book is dedicated to Mark Roberts, who for almost forty years has been a partner in ministry, a mentor, a counselor, a hiking buddy, and above all, a very best friend.

NOTES

INTRODUCTION

[1]Scott Cormode, "A People Entrusted to Your Care," *Fuller Studio*, accessed August 10, 2019, https://fullerstudio.fuller.edu/a-people-entrusted-to -your-care.

[2]Edwin H. Friedman, *A Failure of Nerve: Leadership in the Age of the Quick Fix* (New York: Church Publishing, 2017), loc. 3344, Kindle.

[3]Drew Hanson, "Mahalia Jackson and King's Improvisation," *New York Times*, August 28, 2013, www.nytimes.com/2013/08/28/opinion/mahalia-jackson -and-kings-rhetorical-improvisation.html.

1. THE CRISES OF LEADING CHANGE:

[1]Tod Bolsinger, *Canoeing the Mountains: Christian Leadership in Uncharted Territory*, exp. ed. (Downers Grove, IL: InterVarsity Press, 2015), 42.

[2]"No Patent Suit Against People Who Use Our Tech in Good Faith: Elon Musk," *NDTV*, February 2, 2019, www.ndtv.com/world-news/elon-musk-releases -all-tesla-patents-to-help-save-the-earth-1986450; and "Tesla's Free-to-Use Patents Are All About Sustainability—and Strength," *Driven*, February 4, 2019, https://thedriven.io/2019/02/04/tesla-patents-free-to-use-sustainable -strength.

[3]I have written extensively about adaptive leadership in *Canoeing the Mountains*. See also Ronald A. Heifetz and Marty Linsky, *Leadership on the Line: Staying Alive Through the Dangers of Leading* (Boston: Harvard Business School Press, 2002), 13.

[4]Bolsinger, *Canoeing the Mountains*, 19.

[5]See Ronald A. Heifetz, Marty Linsky, and Alexander Grashow, *The Practice of Adaptive Leadership: Tools and Tactics for Changing Your Organization and the World* (Cambridge, MA: Harvard Business School, 2009), loc. 340, Kindle.

[6]"For, whether we are considering a family, a work system, or an entire nation, the resistance that sabotages a leader's initiative usually has less to do with the 'issue' that ensues than with the fact that the leader took initiative." Edwin H. Friedman, *A Failure of Nerve: Leadership in the Age of the Quick Fix* (New York: Church Publishing, 2017), loc. 130.

[7]Friedman, *Failure of Nerve*, loc. 63.

[8]Heifetz, *Leadership on the Line*, 11-12.

[9]Friedman, *Failure of Nerve*, loc. 4365.

[10]Friedman, *Failure of Nerve*, loc. 50.

[11]Bolsinger, *Canoeing in the Mountains*, 170.

[12]Scott D. Anthony, Clark G. Gilbert, Mark W. Johnson, *Dual Transformation: How to Reposition Today's Business While Creating the Future* (Cambridge, MA: Harvard Business Review Press, 2017), loc. 2761, Kindle.

[13]David Hanna, "How GM Destroyed Its Saturn Success," *Forbes*, March 8, 2020, www.forbes.com/2010/03/08/saturn-gm-innovation-leadership-managing -failure.html#1b389d9b6ee3.

[14]Jonathan Sacks, *Lessons in Leadership: A Weekly Reading of the Jewish Bible* (New York: Toby Press, 2015), loc. 265, Kindle.

[15]"Rather than standing out from others (differentiation), a person may stand outside of their circle (cutoff). Genuine separateness is differentiation within a relationship, not independence of it. Cutoff is an exaggeration of the need to be separate—'I can only count on myself' or 'I'll do it alone.' Again, the difference between people who cut off and those who take strong positions is in their functioning. Cutoff is reactive. It's an automatic defense." Peter L. Steinke, *Congregational Leadership in Anxious Times: Being Calm and Courageous No Matter What* (Lanham, MD: Rowman & Littlefield, 2006), 27.

[16]Friedman, *Failure of Nerve*, 27.

[17]"In the moment of crisis, you will not rise to the occasion; you will default to your training." Bolsinger, *Canoeing in the Mountains*, 32.

2. RESILIENCE

[1]For the entire text of both the open letter and the "Letter from Birmingham Jail," see The Martin Luther King, Jr. Research and Education Institute at Stanford University, https://kinginstitute.stanford.edu/king-papers /documents/letter-birmingham-jail and https://teachingamericanhistory .org/library/document/letter-to-martin-luther-king/, accessed July 29, 2020.

[2]Debra A. Roy, "The Good Friday Parade: Birmingham—April 12, 1963, SCO-TUSblog, August 28, 2013, www.scotusblog.com/2013/08/the-good-friday -parade-birmingham-april-12-1963.

[3]"The end is reconciliation, the end is redemption, the end is the creation of the Beloved Community." Martin Luther King Jr., quoted in Marshall Frady, *Martin Luther King, Jr.*, Penguin Lives Biographies (New York: Penguin, 2005), loc. 548, Kindle.

[4]Martin Luther King Jr., "Letter from Birmingham Jail," cited in Martin Luther King Jr., *Why We Can't Wait*, King Legacy 4 (Boston: Beacon Press, 2000), 99.

[5]King, "Letter from Birmingham Jail," cited in King, *Why We Can't Wait*, 96.

[6]King, "Letter from Birmingham Jail," cited in King, *Why We Can't Wait*, 102, 105.

[7]"I feel that non-violence is really the only way that we can follow because violence is just so self-defeating . . . you can through violence burn down a building but you can't establish justice. . . . You can murder a hater, but you can't murder hate. And what we are trying to get rid of this hate and injustice and all these other things that continue the long night of man's inhumanity to man." Martin Luther King Jr., "King in 1967: My Dream Has 'Turned into a Nightmare,'" interview by Sander Vanocur, *NBC News*, May 8, 1967, www.nbcnews.com/news/other/king-1967-my-dream-has-turned-nightmare-f8C11013179.

[8]Andrew Zolli, *Resilience: Why Things Bounce Back* (New York: Free Press, 2012), 7; emphasis added.

[9]Matt Bloom, "Flourishing in Ministry: Clergy, Ministry Life and Wellbeing," Flourishing in Ministry Project, 2017, https://workwellresearch.com/media/images/FIM_Report_Flourishing_in_Ministry_2.pdf; see also "Well Being," University of Notre Dame, accessed August 17, 2019, https://wellbeing.nd.edu.

[10]Doris Kearns Goodwin, *Leadership: In Turbulent Times* (New York: Simon & Schuster, 2018), loc. 80, Kindle.

[11]Richard Blackburn, "Healthy Congregations" (workshop sponsored by Lombard Mennonite Peace Center, Lombard, IL, hosted by Trinity Presbyterian Church, Santa Ana, CA, 2006), cited in Tod Bolsinger, *Canoeing the Mountains: Christian Leadership in Uncharted Territory*, exp. ed. (Downers Grove, IL: InterVarsity Press, 2015), 128.

[12]Jonathan Sacks, *Lessons in Leadership: A Weekly Reading of the Jewish Bible* (New York: Toby Press, 2015), loc. 265, Kindle.

[13]Warren Bennis and Robert H. Thomas, "Crucibles of Leadership," *Harvard Business Review*, September 2002, https://hbr.org/2002/09/crucibles-of-leadership.

[14]"The affirmation of Jesus as God's Son partakes of messianic associations through the use of Ps 2. Jesus, now anointed with the Spirit (cf. Ps 2:2), is through this ceremony of inauguration (cf. the coronation of the king as the background of Ps 2) about to enter into his ministry whereby the nations shall become his heritage (cf. Ps 2:8)." D. A. Hagner, *Matthew 1–13*, Word Biblical Commentary 33A (Dallas: Word, 1993), 58.

[15]"Mission and identity are inseparable. In John, not only is there a parallel between the mission of Jesus and his disciples, but there also are parallels between who and what Jesus is and who and what the disciples are: both the disciples' mission and their identity are derivative of and dependent on Jesus' mission and identity." Marianne Meye Thompson, *John: A Commentary*, New Testament Library (Louisville, KY: Westminster John Knox Press, 2015), 421.

[16]"Being known by God is the key to personal identity. If one of the universal desires of the self is to be acknowledged and known by others, then being known by God as his children meets our deepest and lifelong need for recognition and gives us a secure identity." Brian S. Rosner, *Known by God: A Biblical Theology of Personal Identity*, Biblical Theology for Life (Grand Rapids: Zondervan, 2017), 245.

[17]Ruth Haley Barton, *Strengthening the Soul of Your Leadership: Seeking God in the Crucible of Ministry* (Downers Grove, IL: InterVarsity Press, 2018), 83.

[18]See Richard N. Pitt, *Divine Callings: Understanding the Call to Ministry in Black Pentecostalism* (New York: NYU Press, 2012), loc. 922, Kindle; and Tod Bolsinger, "Formed Not Found," *Fuller Studio*, accessed August 19, 2019, https://fullerstudio.fuller.edu/formed-not-found.

[19]See Mark Labberton, *Called: The Crisis and Promise of Following Jesus Today* (Downers Grove, IL: InterVarsity Press, 2014).

[20]See Marty Linsky, "Martin Linsky: Pushing Against the Wind," *Faith & Leadership*, September 27, 2010, www.faithandleadership.com/marty-linsky-pushing-against-wind.

[21]Diane Coutu, "How Resilience Works," *Harvard Business Review*, May 2002 https://hbr.org/2002/05/how-resilience-works.

[22]Jim Collins, *Good to Great and the Social Sectors: A Monograph to Accompany Good to Great* (New York: HarperCollins, 2005), loc. 461-462, Kindle. See also Jim Collins, "The Stockdale Paradox," *Jim Collins* (blog), accessed March 31, 2020, www.jimcollins.com/media_topics/TheStockdaleParadox.html.

[23]Viktor Frankl, cited in Coutu, "How Resilience Works."

[24]Edwin H. Friedman, *A Failure of Nerve: Leadership in the Age of the Quick Fix* (New York: Seabury Books, 2007), locs. 339-44, Kindle.

[25]See Steve Cuss, *Managing Leadership Anxiety* (Nashville: Thomas Nelson, 2019), 119, 122.

[26]"That pull toward peer pressure or people-pleasing—may be moving us, or where our pride is getting in the way. Practicing decision-making at a slower pace allows us to admit, 'Lord I am afraid of what people will think. So I'm going to surrender this and try to hear what you think." Terry Looper, *Sacred Pace* (Nashville: Thomas Nelson, 2019), 145.

3. WORKING

[1]Pierre Gurdjian, Thomas Halbeisen, and Kevin Lane, "Why Leadership-Development Programs Fail," *McKinsey Quarterly*, January 2014, www.mckinsey.com/featured-insights/leadership/why-leadership-development-programs-fail.

[2]Michael Beer, Magnus Finnstrom, and Derek Schrader, "Why Leadership Training Fails—and What to Do About It," *Harvard Business Review*, October

2016, https://hbr.org/2016/10/why-leadership-training-fails-and-what-to-do-about-it.

[3]Beer, Finnstrom, and Schrader, "Why Leadership Training Fails."

[4]"The resulting 'persistence of form' has extraordinary importance for leaders. They must understand that what they are up against goes beyond the way things are organized. The nature of connections in the present can have more to do with what has been transmitted successively for many generations than with the logic of their contemporary relationship. This perspective also has revolutionary implications for the way consultants (whether to families or organizations) tend to operate, since they are constantly trying to fix problems through administrative, technological, or managerial changes—which is what most 'advice' consists of. Unless these structural changes are accompanied by changes in an institution's multigenerational emotional processes, they will almost always regress eventually. Edwin H. Friedman, *A Failure of Nerve: Leadership in the Age of the Quick Fix* (New York: Church Publishing, 2017), loc.4391, Kindle.

[5]Abigail Adams, cited in Doris Kearns Goodwin, *Leadership: In Turbulent Times* (New York: Simon & Schuster, 2018), loc. 80, Kindle.

[6]Bennis and Thomas, "Crucibles of Leadership."

[7]Jonathan Sacks, *Lessons in Leadership: A Weekly Reading of the Jewish Bible* (New York: Toby Press, 2015), loc. 1268, Kindle.

[8]Ronald A. Heifetz, Marty Linsky, and Alexander Grashow, *The Practice of Adaptive Leadership: Tools and Tactics for Changing Your Organization and the World* (Cambridge, MA: Harvard Business School, 2009), loc. 384, Kindle.

[9]Tod Bolsinger, *Canoeing the Mountains: Christian Leadership in Uncharted Territory*, exp. ed. (Downers Grove, IL: InterVarsity Press, 2015), 19.

[10]"The leader in the system is the one who is not blaming anyone" but taking personal responsibility for one's own and the groups' functioning. Edwin Friedman, "A Failure of Nerve: Leadership in the Age of the Quick Fix," lecture given in 1996 in Michigan, cited in Bolsinger, *Canoeing the Mountains*, 21.

[11]Goodwin, *Leadership*, 98.

[12]"Cultural humility is a perspective that involves practicing lifelong learning, exercising self-reflection and critique, recognizing the dynamics of power and privilege, and being comfortable with not knowing." See the home page of Culturally Connected at www.culturallyconnected.ca.

[13]Sacks, *Lessons in Leadership*, loc. 2057.

[14]Here are some books for your own exploration: Daniel Hill, *White Awake: An Honest Look at What It Means to Be White* (Downers Grove, IL: InterVarsity Press, 2017); Austin Channing Brown, *I'm Still Here: Black Dignity in a World Made for Whiteness* (New York: Crown Publishing, 2018); Debby Irving,

Waking Up White: and Finding Myself in the Story of Race (Cambridge, MA: Elephant Room, 2014); Michael Evans, *Leadership in the Black Church: Guidance in the Midst of Changing Demographics* (Ft. Worth: Austin Brothers, 2018); Robin J. DiAngelo, *White Fragility: Why It's So Hard for White People to Talk About Racism* (Boston: Beacon Press, 2018); Sarah Shin, *Beyond Colorblind: Redeeming Our Ethnic Journey* (Downers Grove, IL: InterVarsity Press, 2017).

[15]Sacks, *Lessons in Leadership*, loc. 2847. "The man Moses was highly respected [*gadol meod*, literally, "very great"] in the land of Egypt, in the eyes of Pharaoh's servants and the people" (Ex. 11:3). The second appears in Numbers: "Now the man Moses was very humble [*anav meod*], more so than anyone else on earth" (Num. 12:3). Note the two characteristics, seemingly opposed—great and humble—both of which Moses had in high degree (*meod*, "very"). This is the combination of attributes R. Yoḥanan attributed to God Himself: 'Wherever you find God's greatness, there you find His humility.'" *Lessons in Leadership*, loc. 3267.

[16]Laslo Bock, cited in Jeanine Prime and Elizabeth Salib, "The Best Leaders Are Humble Leaders," *Harvard Business Review*, May 12, 2014, https://hbr.org/2014/05/the-best-leaders-are-humble-leaders.

[17]"Eight Traits of a Healthy Organizational Culture," *Ethix*, October 1, 2009, https://ethix.org/2009/10/01/eight-traits-of-a-healthy-organizational-culture; and Prime and Salib, "Best Leaders Are Humble Leaders."

[18]Sue Shallenberger, "The Best Bosses are Humble Bosses," *Wall Street Journal*, October 9, 2018 www.wsj.com/articles/the-best-bosses-are-humble-bosses-1539092123?mod=e2fb.

[19]Patagonia executive cited in Shallenberger, "Best Bosses are Humble Bosses"; emphasis added.

[20]"Mirror Neuron," *Wikipedia*, accessed April 1, 2020, https://en.wikipedia.org/wiki/Mirror_neuron.

[21]"We believe that great leaders are those whose behavior powerfully leverages the system of brain interconnectedness." *HBR's 10 Must Reads on Collaboration: Featuring "Social Intelligence and the Biology of Leadership" by Daniel Goleman and Richard Boyatzis* (Cambridge, MA: Harvard Business Review Press, 2013), 15.

[22]Tomas Chamorro-Premuzic, "Can You Really Improve Your Emotional Intelligence?" *Harvard Business Review*, May 29, 2013. https://hbr.org/2013/05/can-you-really-improve-your-em.

[23]Daniel Goleman, *Leadership: The Power of Emotional Intelligence* (Northampton, MA: More Than Sound, 2011), loc. 341, Kindle.

[24]Roy M. Oswald and Arland Jacobson, *The Emotional Intelligence of Jesus: Relational Smarts for Religious Leaders* (Lanham, MD: Rowman & Littlefield, 2015), loc. 204, Kindle.

[25]Brené Brown, "Brené Brown on Empathy," *YouTube*, December 10, 2013, www
.youtube.com/watch?time_continue=19&v=1Evwgu369Jw.

[26]Charles Duhigg, "What Google Learned from Its Quest to Build the Perfect
Team," *New York Times Magazine*, February 25, 2016, www.nytimes.com/2016
/02/28/magazine/what-google-learned-from-its-quest-to-build-the
-perfect-team.html.

[27]Goleman, *Leadership*, loc. 467.

[28]Jim Herrington and Trisha Taylor, "The Importance of Emotional Intelligence," *The Leader's Journey Podcast*, September 11, 2018, https://theleaders
journey.us/ep6.

[29]Chris Voss, *Never Split the Difference: Negotiating As If Your Life Depended On
It* (New York: HarperCollins, 2016), 52.

[30]Voss, *Never Split the Difference*, 52.

[31]Kim Scott, *Radical Candor: Be a Kick-Ass Boss Without Losing Your Humanity*
(New York: St. Martin's Press, 2018).

[32]Marty Linsky, "Pushing Against the Wind," *Faith & Leadership*, September 27,
2010, www.faithandleadership.com/marty-linsky-pushing-against-wind.

[33]"It is our suggestion that when asked what should be done with this woman,
Jesus stooped to write with his finger on the ground to give him time to
figure out how to manage this emotionally charged situation." Roy M.
Oswald and Arland Jacobson, *The Emotional Intelligence of Jesus: Relational
Smarts for Religious Leaders* (Lanham, MD: Rowman & Littlefield, 2015), loc.
142-143.

[34]Diane Coutu, "How Resilience Works," *Harvard Business Review*, May 2002
https://hbr.org/2002/05/how-resilience-works.

[35]Henry Cloud, *Integrity: The Courage to Meet the Demands of Reality* (New York:
HarperCollins, 2009), 24.

[36]Andrew Zolli, *Resilience: Why Things Bounce Back* (New York: Free Press,
2012), 13; emphasis added.

[37]"Most real change is not about change. It's about identifying what cultural
DNA is worth conserving, is precious and essential, and that indeed makes
it worth suffering the losses so that you can find a way to bring the best of
your tradition and history and values into the future." Ronald A. Heifetz,
"Leadership, Adaptability, Thriving," *Faith & Leadership*, November 18, 2009,
www.youtube.com/watch?v=CSZId1VlYxc.

[38]Coutu, "How Resilience Works."

[39]"More than anyone else in Genesis, Jacob is surrounded by conflict: not just
between himself and Esau, but between himself and Laban, between Rachel
and Leah, and between his children, Joseph and his brothers. It is as if the
Torah were telling us that so long as there is a conflict within us, there will

be a conflict around us. We have to resolve the tension in ourselves before we can do so for others." Sacks, *Lessons in Leadership*, loc. 887-899.

[40] Karl Moore, "Agility: The Ingredient That Will Define Next Generation Leadership," *Forbes Online*, June 12, 2012, https://www.forbes.com/sites/karlmoore /2012/06/12/agility-the-ingredient-that-will-define-next-generation-leadership.

[41] This concept comes from management author Jim Collins, who wrote, "The great paradox of change is that the organizations that best adapt to a changing world first and foremost know what should not change; they have a fixed anchor of guiding principles around which they can more easily change everything else," Jim Collins, "And the Walls Came Tumbling Down," 1999, www.jim collins.com/article_topics/articles/and-the-walls.html, accessed April 17, 2020.

[42] Edwin H. Friedman, *A Failure of Nerve: Leadership in the Age of the Quick Fix* (New York: Church Publishing, 2017), loc. 3338, Kindle.

[43] Friedman, *Failure of Nerve*, loc. 3338.

[44] "An increasing body of empirical evidence shows that resilience—whether in children, survivors of concentration camps, or businesses back from the brink—can be learned." Coutu, "How Resilience Works."

[45] Angela Duckworth, *Grit: The Power of Passion and Perseverance* (New York: Simon & Schuster, 2018), loc. 198, Kindle.

[46] "Even more than the effort a gritty person puts in on a single day, what matters is that they wake up the next day, and the next, ready to get on that treadmill and keep going." Duckworth, *Grit*, loc. 793.

[47] Duckworth's work has come under some scrutiny for what feels like an obvious blind spot to structural poverty, including the social and economic differences that make it possible for some to be able to give themselves to the kind of focused, disciplined passion that scores well on a grit scale. In addition, studies of early childhood stress reveal that the home life, emotional support ,and economic stability of a young child is actually more determinative of later success than most other factors. See David Denby, "The Limits of 'Grit,'" *New Yorker*, June 21, 2016, www.newyorker.com/culture /culture-desk/the-limits-of-grit. Duckworth's own "gritty" response to this criticism has been to acknowledge where her research has overstated the results, to pay more attention to criticism offered (including becoming part of the dissertation committee of one of her critics to learn more about the effects of structural poverty on measures of success), and to add more emphasis on character formation in her ongoing work. "Sometimes, I think people believe that I or others see grit as the only thing kids need to be successful and happy. In fact, I think character is a very long list of things that kids need to be happy and productive. It's not just grit. It's also curiosity. It's not just curiosity. It's also gratitude and kindness. It's not just that. It's emo-

tional and social intelligence. It's not just that. It's open-mindedness. It's not just that. It's honesty. It's not just that. It's humility. I think when we are talking about what kids need to grow up to live lives that are happy and healthy and good for other people, it's a long list of things. Grit is on that list, but it is not the only thing on the list. I'll tell you, as a mother, but also as a scientist and as a former teacher, that it's not the first thing on the list either." See Angela Duckworth, cited in Jeffrey R. Young, "Angela Duckworth Says Grit Is Not Enough. She's Building Tools to Boost Student Character," *EdSurge*, April 20, 2018, www.edsurge.com/news/2018-04-20-angela-duckworth-says-grit-is-not-enough-she-s-building-tools-to-boost-student-character.

[48]David Brooks, "Putting Grit in Its Place," *New York Times*, May 10, 2016, www.nytimes.com/2016/05/10/opinion/putting-grit-in-its-place.html?nytmobile=0.

[49]Viktor E. Frankl, *Man's Search for Meaning* (Boston: Beacon Press, 2006), 103-4.

[50]"10,000 hours of deliberate practice" is the famous (and controversial) metric developed by Anders Ericsson and made famous by Malcolm Gladwell. See Malcolm Gladwell, *Outliers: The Story of Success* (New York: Little, Brown, 2008). Cf. Daniel Coyle, *The Talent Code: Greatness Isn't Born It's Grown* (New York: Random House, 2009), 47. See also "Deliberate practice is characterized by several elements, each worth examining. It is activity designed specifically to improve performance, often with a teacher's help; it can be repeated a lot; feedback on results is continuously available; it's highly demanding mentally, whether the activity is purely intellectual, such as chess or business-related activities, or heavily physical, such as sports; and it isn't much fun." Geoff Colvin, *Talent Is Overrated: What Really Separates World-Class Performers from Everybody Else* (New York: Penguin, 2010), 66.

[51]Duckworth, *Grit*, loc. 1346.

[52]"We learned that quality collaboration does not begin with relationships and trust; it starts with a focus on individual motivation." Carlos Valdes-Dapena, "Stop Wasting Money on Team Building," *Harvard Business Review*, September 11, 2018, https://hbr.org/2018/09/stop-wasting-money-on-team-building.

[53]David Brooks, "Students Learn from People They Love," *New York Times*, January 17, 2019, www.nytimes.com/2019/01/17/opinion/learning-emotion-education.html.

[54]Eric Schmidt, *Trillion Dollar Coach* (New York: HarperBusiness, 2019), 172.

[55]See Luke 8:15; Luke 21:19; Romans 5:3; Romans 15:4; 2 Corinthians 6:4; 2 Corinthians 12:12; Colossians 1:11; 2 Thessalonians 1:4; 1 Timothy 6:11; 2 Timothy 3:10; Titus 2:2; Hebrews 10:36; James 1:3; James 5:11; 2 Peter 1:6; Revelation 2:2f, 19; Revelation 13:10; Revelation 14:12.

[56]Martin Luther King Jr., *Why We Can't Wait*, King Legacy 4 (Boston: Beacon Press, 2010), 69-70.

4. HEATING

[1]"SWOT" analysis is a business strategy tool for assessing an organization's Strengths, Weaknesses, Opportunities, and Threats.

[2]Manish Chopra, "Want to Be a Better Leader? Observe More and React Less," *McKinsey Quarterly*, February 2016, www.mckinsey.com/featured-insights /leadership/want-to-be-a-better-leader-observe-more-and-react-less.

[3]John Dewey, cited in Tod Bolsinger, *Canoeing the Mountains: Christian Leadership in Uncharted Territory*, exp. ed. (Downers Grove, IL: InterVarsity Press, 2015), 22.

[4]Edwin H. Friedman, *A Failure of Nerve: Leadership in the Age of the Quick Fix* (New York: Church Publishing, 2017), loc. 3340, Kindle; emphasis added.

[5]Dwight Zscheile, *The Agile Church: Spirit-Led Innovation in an Uncertain Age* (New York: Church Publishing, 2014), loc. 1518-1519, Kindle.

[6]"The Three Hardest Words in the English Language (Ep. 167): Full Transcript," *Freakonomics*, May 15, 2014, http://freakonomics.com/2014/05/15/the -three-hardest-words-in-the-english-language-full-transcript.

[7]Ronald A Heifetz, *Leadership Without Easy Answers* (Cambridge, MA: Harvard University Press, 1998), 2.

[8]Tomas Chamorro-Premuzic, "Why Do So Many Incompetent Men Become Leaders?" *Harvard Business Review*, August 22, 2013, https://hbr.org/2013/08/why -do-so-many-incompetent-men.

[9]Warren Bennis and Robert H. Thomas, "Crucibles of Leadership," *Harvard Business Review*, September 2002, https://hbr.org/2002/09/crucibles-of-leadership.

[10]Martin Luther King Jr., quoted in Marshall Frady, *Martin Luther King, Jr.*, Penguin Lives Biographies (New York: Penguin, 2005), loc. 594, Kindle.

[11]King, quoted in Frady, *Martin Luther King, Jr.*, loc. 617.

[12]Lynn Ziegenfuss, face-to-face interview with author, December 17, 2018.

[13]Mark Roberts, face-to-face interview with author, Pasadena, CA, August 28, 2019.

[14]Friedman, *Failure of Nerve*, loc. 3338.

[15]For a history of the Society of Jesus and their remarkable accomplishments, see Chris Lowney, *Heroic Leadership: Best Practices from a 450-year-old Company That Changed the World* (Chicago: Loyola Press, 2005), 7-8.

[16]Lowney, *Heroic Leadership*, 29.

[17]Lowney, *Heroic Leadership*, 97-98, emphasis mine.

[18]Lowney, *Heroic Leadership*, 27, emphasis mine.

[19]Jerry Colonna, *Reboot: Leadership and the Art of Growing Up* (Cambridge, MA: HarperBusiness. 2019), loc. 154-155, Kindle.

[20]Brené Brown, *Dare to Lead* (New York: Random House, 2018), 19.

[21]Brené Brown, "The Power of Vulnerability," TEDxHouston, June 2010, www.ted.com/talks/brene_brown_on_vulnerability/transcript.

[22]Brené Brown, *Daring Greatly* (New York: Avery Publishing, 2015), 2.

[23]"A rumble is a discussion, conversation, or meeting defined by a commitment to lean into vulnerability, to stay curious and generous, to stick with the messy middle of problem identification and solving, to take a break and circle back when necessary, to be fearless in owning our parts, and, as psychologist Harriet Lerner teaches, to listen with the same passion with which we want to be heard. More than anything else, when someone says, 'Let's rumble,' it cues me to show up with an open heart and mind so we can serve the work and each other, not our egos." Brown, *Dare to Lead*, 10.

[24]"I want to experience your vulnerability but I don't want to be vulnerable. Vulnerability is courage in you and inadequacy in me." Brown, *Daring Greatly*, 41-42.

[25]Jonathan Sacks, *Lessons in Leadership* (New Milford, CT: Maggid, 2015), loc. 802, Kindle.

[26]Sacks, *Lessons in Leadership*, loc. 802.

[27]Sacks, *Lessons in Leadership*, loc. 822.

[28]Brown, *Dare to Lead*, 30.

[29]Brown, *Dare to Lead*, 10.

[30]Jimmy Mellado, interview with author at Fuller Seminary, October 19, 2018.

[31]Lowney, *Heroic Leadership*, 96.

[32]Ronald A. Heifetz, Marty Linsky, and Alexander Grashow, *The Practice of Adaptive Leadership: Tools and Tactics for Changing Your Organization and the World* (Cambridge, MA: Harvard Business School, 2009), loc. 267, Kindle; emphasis added.

[33]See Brené Brown, "The Call to Courage," *Netflix*, April 19, 2019, www.netflix.com/title/81010166.

[34]For a good, accessible introduction to both the prayer of examen and the entire *Spiritual Exercises*, see Kevin O'Brien, *The Ignatian Adventure: Experiencing the Spiritual Exercises of St. Ignatius in Daily Life* (Chicago: Loyola Press, 2011), 75.

[35]O'Brien, *Ignatian Adventure*, 78.

[36]I heartily recommend this online resource from the British Jesuits for the prayer of examen: "Examen Prayer," *Pray as You Go*, accessed April 2, 2020, https://pray-as-you-go.org/retreat/examen-prayer.

5. HOLDING

[1]Kevass J Harding, *Can These Bones Live?* (Nashville: Abingdon Press, 2007), xiii.

[2]Interview with the author, August 20, 2019.

[3]Joseph M. Marshall, *Keep Going: The Art of Perseverance* (New York: Sterling Ethos, 2009), loc.70, Kindle.

[4]C. Kavin Rowe, "Cultivating Resilience in Christ-Shaped Leaders," *Faith and Leadership*, April 23, 2012, https://faithandleadership.com/c-kavin-rowe -cultivating-resilience-christ-shaped-leaders.

[5]"Don't Quit on Me: What Young People Who Left School Say About the Power of Relationships," America's Promise Alliance, September 6, 2015, www.grad nation.org/report/dont-quit-me.

[6]"A Navy SEAL Explains 8 Secrets to Grit and Resilience," *Barking Up the Wrong Tree*, accessed September 7, 2019, www.bakadesuyo.com/2015/01/grit.

[7]William A. Barry, a Jesuit priest and author writes, "Prayer is a matter of relationship. Intimacy is the basic issue, not answers to problems or resolutions 'to be better.' Many of life's problems and challenges have no answers; we can only live with and through them. Problems and challenges, however, can be faced and lived through with more peace and resilience if people know that they are not alone." William A. Barry, cited in O'Brien, *Ignatian Adventure*, 96.

[8]Daniel Smith et al., "The Will to Lead: Grit and Resilience in Senior Leadership," paper read at unidentified conference, April 2018, www.researchgate .net/publication/321873931_The_Will_to_Lead_Grit_and_Resilience_in _Senior_Leadership.

[9]Jonathan Sacks, *Lessons in Leadership: A Weekly Reading of the Jewish Bible* (New York: Toby Press, 2015), loc.3153, Kindle.

[10]Eric Schmidt, *Trillion Dollar Coach* (New York: HarperBusiness, 2019), 23; emphasis added.

[11]Mark Roberts, face-to-face interview with author, Pasadena, CA, August 29, 2019.

[12]Erving Goffman, *The Presentation of the Self in Everyday Life* (New York: Anchor books, 1959), 141.

[13]Matt Bloom, "The Stages of Ministry: Research Insights from the Flourishing in Ministry Project," Flourishing in Ministry Project, July 2017, https://work-wellresearch.com/media/images/FIM%20Report%20Stages%20of%20Min-istry_YusOEKp.pdf.

[14]Ronald Heifetz, quoted in "The Leader of the Future: An Interview with Ronald Heifetz," interview by William C. Taylor, *Fast Company*, May 31, 1999, www.fastcompany.com/37229/leader-future.

[15]Tod Bolsinger, *Canoeing the Mountains: Christian Leadership in Uncharted Territory*, exp. ed. (Downers Grove, IL: InterVarsity Press, 2015), 242. Cf. Ronald A. Heifetz, Marty Linsky, and Alexander Grashow, *The Practice of Adaptive Leadership: Tools and Tactics for Changing Your Organization and the World* (Cambridge, MA: Harvard Business School, 2009), chap. 10.

[16]Bolsinger, *Canoeing the Mountains*, 160.

[17]Heifetz, Linsky, and Grashow, *Practice of Adaptive Leadership*, loc. 2282.

[18]Margaret J. Wheatley, "When Change Is Out of Control," *Margaret J. Wheatley*, accessed September 6, 2019, www.margaretwheatley.com/articles/whenchange isoutofcontrol.html.

[19]The insights from this study, while never published, became part of both Ziegenfuss's and Wright's own work as trainers, mentors, spiritual director (Ziegenfuss) and the executive director of a leadership center (Wright), and in Wright's book *Relational Leadership: A Biblical Model for Influence and Service* (Milton Keynes, UK: Paternoster, 2000), loc. 746-749, Kindle. Lynn Ziegenfuss and Walter Wright, interview with author, Pasadena, CA, December 17, 2018.

[20]Wright, *Relational Leadership*, loc. 746-749.

[21]Sacks, *Lessons in Leadership*, loc. 1503.

[22]"I have contended in the past that Moses neither sinned nor was punished. He merely acted as he had done almost forty years earlier when God told him to hit the rock (Ex. 17:6), and thereby showed that though he was the right leader for the people who had been slaves in Egypt, he was not the leader for their children who were born in freedom and would conquer the land." Sacks, *Lessons in Leadership*, loc. 3122.

[23]Sacks, *Lessons in Leadership*, loc. 3138, 3148.

[24]Harry Mills and Mark Dombreck, "Resilience: Relationships," *MentalHelp.net*, accessed February 14, 2018, www.mentalhelp.net/articles/resilience-relationships. "Resilience depends on supportive, responsive relationships and mastering a set of capabilities that can help us respond and adapt to adversity in healthy ways," says Jack Shonkoff, director of the Center on the Developing Child at Harvard. "It's those capacities and relationships that can turn toxic stress into tolerable stress." Bari Walsh, "The Science of Resilience." Harvard Graduate School of Education, March 23, 2015, www.gse.harvard.edu/news/uk /15/03/science-resilience.

[25]Heifetz, quoted in Taylor, "The Leader of the Future."

[26]Bolsinger, *Canoeing the Mountains*, 160.

6. HAMMERING

[1]"As defined, deliberate practice is a very specialized form of practice. You need a teacher or coach who assigns practice techniques designed to help you improve on very specific skills. That teacher or coach must draw from a highly developed body of knowledge about the best way to teach these skills." Anders Ericsson, *Peak: Secrets from the New Science of Expertise* (New York: Houghton Mifflin Harcourt, 2016), 100. See also Angela Duckworth,

Grit: The Power of Passion and Perseverance (New York: Simon & Schuster, 2018), chap. 7; and Angela Duckworth, "Duckworth: 'Deliberate Practice' Is an Important Element of Grit," *Education Dive*, April 18, 2018, www.educationdive .com/news/duckworth-deliberate-practice-is-an-important-element -of-grit/521559.

[2]Steve Yamaguchi, quoted in Tod Bolsinger, *Canoeing the Mountains: Christian Leadership in Uncharted Territory*, exp. ed. (Downers Grove, IL: InterVarsity Press, 2015), 32.

[3]"Somewhat ironically, perhaps, all of the 'spiritual' disciplines are, or essentially involve, bodily behaviors. But really, that makes perfect sense. For the body is the first field of energy beyond our thoughts that we have direction over, and all else we influence is due to our power over it. Moreover, it is the chief repository of the wrong habits that we must set aside, as well as the place where new habits are to be instituted. We are, within limits, able to command it to do things that will transform our habits—especially the inner habits of thought and feeling—and so enable us to do things not now in our power." Dallas Willard, *The Divine Conspiracy: Rediscovering Our Hidden Life in God* (New York: HarperCollins, 2014), 353-54.

[4]Willard, *Divine Conspiracy*, 353.

[5]See Donald B. Kraybill, Steven M. Nolt, and David L. Weaver-Zercher, *Amish Grace* (San Francisco: John Wiley, 2007). Cf. Mark Berman, "'I Forgive You.' Relatives of Charleston Church Shooting Victims Address Dylann Roof," *Washington Post*, June 19, 2015, www.washingtonpost.com/news/post -nation/wp/2015/06/19/i-forgive-you-relatives-of-charleston-church -victims-address-dylann-roof/.

[6]See Mark Lau Branson, "Defining Disciplines and Practices," Fuller Seminary, accessed September 10, 2019, https://vimeo.com/317111827. See also Dorothy Bass, ed., *Practicing Our Faith: A Way of Life for a Searching People*, Practices of Faith (San Francisco: John Wiley, 2020), which states: "Christian practices are things Christian people do together over time in response to and in the light of God's active presence for the life of the world in Christ Jesus."

[7]Stephen A. Macchia, *Crafting a Rule of Life: An Invitation to the Well-Ordered Way* (Downers Grove, IL: InterVarsity Press, 2012), loc. 129, Kindle.

[8]"Benedictine stability clearly complemented the monastic regimen of daily communal prayer at fixed hours. Centuries later, Loyola and the Jesuits would find little value in stability, or in communal prayer at set times. Instead, Jesuit prayer was individual, on-the-go, and self-regulating—like the examen. . . . While Benedict's monks pronounced a vow of stability, remaining in one monastery for life, Jesuits were instead committed to mobility. Loyola's lieutenant Jeronimo Nadal barnstormed Europe framing the

distinctive Jesuit mindset and lifestyle: '[Jesuits] realize that they cannot build or acquire enough houses to be able from nearby to run out to the combat. Since that is the case, they consider that they are in their most peaceful and pleasant house when they are constantly on the move, when they travel throughout the earth, when they have no place to call their own.'" Chris Lowney, *Heroic Leadership: Best Practices from a 450-year-old Company That Changed the World* (Chicago: Loyola Press, 2005), 141, 146.

[9]Martin Luther King Jr., *Why We Can't Wait*, King Legacy 4 (Boston: Beacon Press, 2000), 69-70.

[10]Lauren A. Keating, Peter A. Heslin, and Susan J. Ashford, "Good Leaders Are Good Learners," *Harvard Business Review*, August 10, 2017, https://hbr.org/2017/08/good-leaders-are-good-learners.

[11]See Eric Schmidt, *Trillion Dollar Coach* (New York: HarperBusiness, 2019). Cf. Jennifer Reingold, "The Secret Coach," *CNN Money*, July 21, 208, https://money.cnn.com/2008/07/21/technology/reingold_coach.fortune/index.htm.

[12]Ericsson, *Peak*, 100.

[13]Peter A. Heslin and Lauren A. Keating, "In Learning Mode? The Role of Mindsets in Derailing and Enabling Experiential Leadership Development," *Leadership Quarterly* 28, no 3 (June 2017): 367-84, www.sciencedirect.com/science/article/pii/S1048984316301345?via%3Dihub. The seminal work on this topic is from Carol Dweck, who described having a "growth mindset" as "the belief that your basic qualities are things you can cultivate through your efforts, your strategies, and help from others. Although people may differ in every which way—in their initial talents and aptitudes, interests, or temperaments—everyone can change and grow through application and experience." Carol S. Dweck, *Mindset* (New York: Random House, 2016), 7. See also Carol Dweck, "The Power of Believing You Can Improve," *TEDxNorrkoping*, accessed October 5, 2019, www.ted.com/talks/carol_dweck_the_power_of_believing_that_you_can_improve.

[14]Lynn Ziegenfuss and Walter Wright, Leading Change Doctor of Ministry Cohort presentation and discussion, Fuller Theological Seminary, Pasadena, CA, June 18, 2019.

[15]Lynn Ziegenfuss, face-to-face interview with author, Pasadena, CA, December 9, 2016.

[16]"I encourage leaders to escape the expert expectation by becoming an expert experimenter, an expert question asker instead of answer giver. I often coach my clients, 'Make your goal in every conversation to have someone roll their eyes upward (which indicates that they are thinking differently) and say, "That's a great question."' A great question when asked, and attempted to answer, offers more than a solution—a transformation." Bolsinger, *Canoeing the Mountains*, 213-14.

[17] Jonathan Sacks, *Lessons in Leadership: A Weekly Reading of the Jewish Bible* (New York: Toby Press, 2015), loc. 4422, Kindle.

[18] Scott Cormode, "A People Entrusted to Your Care," *Fuller Studio*, accessed August 10, 2019. https://fullerstudio.fuller.edu/a-people-entrusted-to-your-care.

[19] Henri J. M. Nouwen, *Making All Things New* (New York: HarperOne, 1981), loc. 313, Kindle.

[20] Nouwen, *Making All Things New*, loc. 313.

[21] Ronald A. Heifetz, Marty Linsky, and Alexander Grashow, *The Practice of Adaptive Leadership: Tools and Tactics for Changing Your Organization and the World* (Cambridge, MA: Harvard Business School, 2009), loc. 287, Kindle.

[22] Heifetz, Linsky, and Grashow, *Practice of Adaptive Leadership*, loc. 287.

[23] "The leader's primary responsibility is to make judgment calls." Nick Tasler, *Domino: The Simplest Way to Inspire Change* (San Francisco: John Wiley, 2015), 113.

[24] Daniel Hill, *White Awake: An Honest Look at What It Means to Be White* (Downers Grove, IL: InterVarsity Press, 2017), 155.

[25] Heifetz, Linsky, and Grashow, *Practice of Adaptive Leadership*, loc. 679-82. Cf. Bolsinger, *Canoeing the Mountains*, 111.

[26] Heifetz, Linsky, and Grashow, *Practice of Adaptive Leadership*, loc. 2110.

[27] Heifetz, Linsky, and Grashow, *Practice of Adaptive Leadership*, loc. 295.

[28] "Productive change begins when you have the discipline to confront the brutal facts." Jim Collins, *Turning the Flywheel: A Monograph to Accompany Good to Great* (New York: HarperBusiness, 2010), 33. See also Jim Collins, "Keeping the Flywheel in Motion," *Knowledge Project Podcast*, accessed October 8, 2019, https://fs.blog/jim-collins.

[29] Martin Luther King Jr., "I Have a Dream," Address Delivered at the March on Washington for Jobs and Freedom," Stanford University, accessed October 7, 2019, https://kinginstitute.stanford.edu/king-papers/documents/i-have-dream-address-delivered-march-washington-jobs-and-freedom.

[30] Soong-Chan Rah, *Prophetic Lament: A Call for Justice in Troubled Times* (Downers Grove, IL: InterVarsity Press, 2015), 22.

[31] Rah, *Prophetic Lament*, 21.

[32] "The Psalms of Lament," Fuller Seminary, www.youtube.com/watch?v=dXyuLxqAw88, accessed April 17, 2020.

[33] Bryan Stevenson quoted in Leandra Fernandez, "Empathy and Social Justice: The Power of Proximity in Improvement Science," Carnegie Foundation, April 21, 2016, www.carnegiefoundation.org/blog/empathy-and-social-justice-the-power-of-proximity-in-improvement-science.

[34] Jim Collins, "Confront the Brutal Facts," www.jimcollins.com/concepts/confront-the-brutal-facts.html, accessed April 17, 2020.

[35]Collins, *Turning the Flywheel*, 33.

[36]King, "I Have a Dream."

[37]"Father, if you are willing, remove this cup from me; yet, not my will but yours be done" (Luke 22:42).

[38]Christine Lee, video conference conversation with author, October 10, 2019.

[39]King, "I Have a Dream."

7. HEWING

[1]Ronald Heifetz, foreword to Jonathan Sacks, *Lessons in Leadership: A Weekly Reading of the Jewish Bible* (New York: Toby Press, 2015), loc. 178, Kindle.

[2]"Adaptive leadership is the practice of mobilizing people to tackle tough challenges and thrive." Ronald A. Heifetz, Marty Linsky, and Alexander Grashow, *The Practice of Adaptive Leadership: Tools and Tactics for Changing Your Organization and the World* (Cambridge, MA: Harvard Business School, 2009), loc. 383, Kindle.

[3]Heifetz, foreword to Sacks, *Lessons in Leadership*, loc. 181.

[4]"If we are willing to go deeper, we will see that white privilege is the legacy of white supremacy. White privilege is the assumption of racial entitlement and the normality of whiteness, something that most of those of us who are white still fail to recognize or resist. The only redemption of the sin of June 17 is to name the sin of racism and to ask ourselves what true repentance means. As the Bible teaches, repentance is much more than saying we are brokenhearted and sorry; it means turning in a totally new direction." Jim Wallis, *America's Original Sin: Racism, White Privilege, and the Bridge to a New America* (Grand Rapids: Baker, 2017), loc. 241, Kindle.

[5]"What Heifetz and his colleagues refer to often as a "holding environment" or "containing vessel" is far more an expression of relationships than a formal configuration of policies, procedures, and rules. "A holding environment consists of all those ties that bind people together and enable them to maintain their collective focus on what they are trying to do. All the human sources of cohesion." Tod Bolsinger, *Canoeing the Mountains: Christian Leadership in Uncharted Territory*, exp. ed. (Downers Grove, IL: InterVarsity Press, 2015), 65. See also, Heifetz, Linsky, Grashow, *Practice of Adaptive Leadership*, loc. 2567-2570.

[6]"For people in authority roles, one of the most difficult aspects of orchestrating conflict is resisting the temptation to take the conflictual elements of the adaptive work off of other people's shoulders and putting it on your own. The pressure to relieve them of that work comes from both them and from you. You have undoubtedly been rewarded for exactly that behavior in

the past. People generally get promoted because they are willing to take problems on their own shoulders and come up with solutions. And people both above and below you are expecting, and prefer, that to continue. They want you to make an authoritative decision that 'resolves' the conflict." Heifetz, Linsky, Grashow, *Practice of Adaptive Leadership*, loc. 2684.

[7]Edwin H. Friedman, *A Failure of Nerve: Leadership in the Age of the Quick Fix* (New York: Church Publishing, 2017), loc. 455-460, Kindle; emphasis added.

[8]The factor that TED Talk curator Chris Anderson says is the key: memorable and actionable communication. See Chris Anderson, "TED's Secret to Great Public Speaking," TED Talk, accessed October 25, 2019, www.ted.com/talks/chris_anderson_teds_secret_to_great_public_speaking.

[9]Alan Mulally, quoted in Carmine Gallo, "Steve Jobs and Alan Mulally Unleashed Innovation with Two Simple Words," *Forbes*, May 16, 2014, www.forbes.com/sites/carminegallo/2014/05/16/steve-jobs-and-alan-mulally-unleashed-innovation-with-two-simple-words/#52379b476275. See also "Leading in the 21st Century: An Interview with Alan Mulally," *McKinsey.com*, November 2013, www.mckinsey.com/business-functions/strategy-and-corporate-finance/our-insights/leading-in-the-21st-century-an-interview-with-fords-alan-mulally.

[10]Like many visionary leaders of different eras, Henry Ford's business vision and foresight is often contrasted with a number of deeply disturbing beliefs, comments, and decisions worthy of condemnation. See "Henry Ford and Anti-Semitism: A Complex Story," *Henry Ford*, accessed February 26, 2020, www.thehenryford.org/collections-and-research/digital-resources/popular-topics/henry-ford-and-anti-semitism-a-complex-story. In addition, recently Ford's very business practices, like the creation of the assembly line, has come under critique for its role in the dehumanization of labor.

[11]See Alan Mulally, "Alan Mulally: Producing Cars with Passion and Involvement," interview by Al Erisman, *Ethix*, July 15, 2010, https://ethix.org/2010/07/15/producing-cars-with-passion-and-involvement. "The first thing that I wanted to do was to pull everybody together around a compelling vision, and I found that in Henry Ford's original vision. It was best characterized by a full-page advertisement that he ran on January 24, 1925, and the headline was 'Opening the highways to all mankind.' He talked about a grand business, safe and efficient transportation, making great products, and contributing to a better world. Henry Ford was the first one to make an electric car. He was also the first one to run cars on biofuels. He also manufactured using 80 percent recycled material. He was at the center of economic growth, energy independence, and a strong environment."

[12]Gallo, "Steve Jobs and Alan Mulally."

[13]For an accessible introduction to these concepts see Daniel Kahneman, *Thinking, Fast and Slow* (New York: Farrar, Straus and Giroux, 2013).

[14]"In the same way that each person is different with a unique DNA, each congregation has its own organizational DNA that affects its relationships and purpose." Bolsinger, *Canoeing the Mountains*, 104.

[15]Eric Ries, *The Lean Startup: How Today's Entrepreneurs Use Continuous Innovation to Create Radically Successful Businesses* (New York: Crown, 2011), 23.

[16]Chip Heath and Dan Heath, *Switch: How to Change Things When Change Is Hard* (New York: Crown, 2010), 53.

[17]Heath and Heath, *Switch*, 53-54.

[18]Eric Schmidt, *Trillion Dollar Coach* (New York: HarperBusiness, 2019), 113-14.

[19]Derek Sivers, "How to Start a Movement," TED2010, accessed April 7, 2020, www.ted.com/talks/derek_sivers_how_to_start_a_movement?language=en#t-154472.

[20]"Jesus' words and actions are resolutely oriented toward glorifying God because they are resolutely oriented toward bringing life to God's world." Marianne Meye Thompson, *John: A Commentary*, New Testament Library (Louisville, KY: Westminster John Knox Press, 2015), 117.

[21]"What transpires in this chapter again echoes the prologue's assertion that the one who was life and light for all the world was received by some and rejected by others." Thompson, *John*, 138.

[22]Friedman, *Failure of Nerve*, loc. 3338.

[23]Jim Singleton, phone interview with author from Ketchum, ID, August 26, 2019.

[24]Cf. Mike Bonem and Roger Patterson, *Leading from the Second Chair*, Jossey-Bass Leadership Network (San Francisco: John Wiley, 2005); and Mike Bonem, *Thriving in the Second Chair* (Nashville: Abingdon Press, 2016).

[25]Friedman, *Failure of Nerve*, loc. 315.

[26]Mike Bonem, phone interview with author, Altadena, CA, September 26, 2019. Mike's two books on second-chair leadership are must-reading for anyone in leadership (in *both* first and second chairs).

[27]Sacks, *Lessons in Leadership*, loc. 1412.

[28]I write about this at some length in my *Canoeing the Mountains*, 22.

8. TEMPERING

[1]"Tempering is usually performed after hardening, to reduce some of the excess hardness, and is done by heating the metal to some temperature below the critical point for a certain period of time, then allowing it to cool in still air. The exact temperature determines the amount of hardness removed, and

depends on both the specific composition of the alloy and on the desired properties in the finished product. For instance, very hard tools are often tempered at low temperatures." "Tempering (metallurgy)," *Wikipedia*, accessed April 7, 2020, https://en.wikipedia.org/wiki/Tempering_(metallurgy).

[2]Shawn Achor and Michelle Gielan, "Resilience Is About How You Recharge, Not How You Endure," *Harvard Business Review*, June 24, 2016, https://hbr.org/2016/06/resilience-is-about-how-you-recharge-not-how-you-endure.

[3]"Bill Bowerman: Nike's Original Innovator," *Nike News*, September 2, 2015, https://news.nike.com/news/bill-bowerman-nike-s-original-innovator.

[4]Bill Bowerman, quoted in Kenny Moore, *Bowermen and the Men of Oregon: The Story of Oregon's Legendary Coach and Nike's Cofounder* (Emmaus, PA: Rodale, 2006), 3.

[5]It's good to remember that God's *resting* on the seventh day of creation, the pattern for our own sabbath, was not because God was tired. God's ceasing of work (an even stronger translation) was for lingering, enjoying, celebrating, and even "walking in the cool of the day" (Genesis 3:8 NIV), being present with God's own creation.

[6]"Mr. Muir, someone told me you did not approve of the word "hike." Is that so?' His blue eyes flashed, and with his Scotch accent he replied: 'I don't like either the word or the thing. People ought to saunter in the mountains—not hike!'

'Do you know the origin of that word "saunter"? It's a beautiful word. Away back in the Middle Ages people used to go on pilgrimages to the Holy Land, and when people in the villages through which they passed asked where they were going, they would reply, "A la sainte terre," "To the Holy Land." And so they became known as sainte-terre-ers or saunterers. Now these mountains are our Holy Land, and we ought to saunter through them reverently, not "hike" through them." Albert W. Palmer, "A Parable of Sauntering," *Sierra Club*, accessed October 25, 2019, https://vault.sierraclub.org/john_muir_exhibit/life/palmer_sauntering.aspx.

EPILOGUE

[1]Jim Collins discusses his view that real change starts not in a vision but in a deep look at the brutal facts of a situation. Jim Collins, "Keeping the Flywheel in Motion," *Knowledge Project Podcast*, accessed October 8, 2019, https://fs.blog/jim-collins.

[2]Marty Linsky, "Martin Linsky: Pushing Against the Wind," *Faith & Leadership*, September 27, 2010, www.faithandleadership.com/marty-linsky-pushing-against-wind; emphasis added.

[3]"The first principle of spiritual formation is this: A spiritually formed person loves God and others." Scot McKnight, *Jesus Creed: Loving God, Loving Others* (London: Paraclete Press, 2004), 3.

[4]Tod Bolsinger, "The Jesus Creed: Love God, Love Neighbors," Tod Bolsinger (blog), May 9, 2007, http://bolsinger.blogs.com/weblog/2007/05/the_jesus _creed.html.

[5]Alan Deutschman, *Change or Die: The Three Keys to Change at Work and in Life* (New York: HarperCollins, 2007), loc. 111-112, Kindle.

[6]Deborah Gage, "The Venture Capital Secret: 3 Out of 4 Start-Ups Fail," *Wall Street Journal*, September 20, 2012, www.wsj.com/articles/SB100008723963 90443720204578004980476429190.

[7]"Why Change Initiatives Fail," UNC Executive Development, November 12, 2015, http://execdev.kenan-flagler.unc.edu/blog/why-change-initiatives-fail.

[8]Ronald A. Heifetz and Marty Linsky, *Leadership on the Line: Staying Alive Through the Dangers of Leading* (Boston: Harvard Business School Press, 2002), loc. 1979, Kindle.

[9]Jonathan Sacks, *Lessons in Leadership: A Weekly Reading of the Jewish Bible* (New York: Toby Press, 2015), loc. 4399, Kindle.

RESOURCES FOR GOING DEEPER

TOD BOLSINGER

TEMPERED RESILIENCE

STUDY GUIDE

8 SESSIONS ON BECOMING AN ADAPTIVE LEADER

For an online course covering content related to this book, go to formation.fuller.edu/courses/resilience.

ALSO BY
TOD BOLSINGER

TOD BOLSINGER

CANOEING

THE

MOUNTAINS

CHRISTIAN

LEADERSHIP IN

UNCHARTED TERRITORY

 Missio Alliance

and

≋ INTERVARSITY PRESS

Missio Alliance has arisen in response to the shared voice of pastors and ministry leaders from across the landscape of North American Christianity for a new "space" of togetherness and reflection amid the issues and challenges facing the church in our day. We are united by a desire for a fresh expression of evangelical faith, one significantly informed by the global evangelical family. Lausanne's Cape Town Commitment, "A Confession of Faith and a Call to Action," provides an excellent guidepost for our ethos and aims.

In partnership with InterVarsity Press, we are pleased to offer a line of resources authored by a diverse range of theological practitioners. The resources in this series are selected based on the important way in which they address and embody these values, and thus, the unique contribution they offer in equipping Christian leaders for fuller and more faithful participation in God's mission.

Available Titles

missioalliance.org | twitter.com/missioalliance | facebook.com/missioalliance

IVP PRAXIS
EQUIPPING LEADERS FOR MINISTRY

God has called us to ministry. But it's not enough to have a vision for ministry if you don't have the practical skills for it. Nor is it enough to do the work of ministry if what you do is headed in the wrong direction. We need both vision *and* expertise for effective ministry. We need *praxis*.

Praxis puts theory into practice. It brings cutting-edge ministry expertise from visionary practitioners. You'll find sound biblical and theological foundations for ministry in the real world, with concrete examples for effective action and pastoral ministry. Praxis books are more than the "how to"—they're also the "why to." And because *being* is every bit as important as *doing*, Praxis attends to the inner life of the leader as well as the outer work of ministry. Feed your soul, and feed your ministry.

If you are called to ministry, you know you can't do it on your own. Let Praxis provide the companions you need to equip God's people for life in the kingdom.

www.ivpress.com/praxis